Mastering the Art of Effective Relationship Communication

Connect Deeply with Your Loved One and Learn the Steps to Communicate Effectively and Create Intimacy

© Copyright 2019 - All rights reserved.

The following book is reproduced below with the goal of providing information that is as accurate and reliable as possible. Regardless, purchasing this book can be seen as consent to the fact that both the publisher and the author of this book are in no way experts on the topics discussed within and that any recommendations or suggestions that are made herein are for entertainment purposes only. Professionals should be consulted as needed prior to undertaking any of the action endorsed herein.

This declaration is deemed fair and valid by both the American Bar Association and the Committee of Publishers Association and is legally binding throughout the United States.

Furthermore, the transmission, duplication, or reproduction of any of the following work including specific information will be considered an illegal act irrespective of if it is done electronically or in print. This extends to creating a secondary or tertiary copy of the work or a recorded copy and is only allowed with the express written consent from the Publisher. All additional rights reserved.

The information in the following pages is broadly considered a truthful and accurate account of facts and as such, any inattention, use, or misuse of the information in question by the reader will render any resulting actions solely under their purview. There are no scenarios in which the publisher or the original author of this work can be in any fashion deemed liable for any hardship or damages that may befall them after undertaking information described herein.

Additionally, the information in the following pages is intended only for informational purposes and should thus be thought of as universal. As befitting its nature, it is presented without assurance regarding its prolonged validity or interim quality. Trademarks that are mentioned are done without written consent and can in no way be considered an endorsement from the trademark holder.

Table of Contents

Introduction 7

Chapter One - Relationships 101 11
    The Vital Needs Every Relationship Must Fulfill 12
    The Five Stages of a Relationship 19

Chapter Two - The Diagnosis 26
    6 Big Signs You and Your Partner Need to Communicate Better 27
    The Reasons Why We Don't Communicate 29
    The 10 Communication Mistakes You Don't Know You're Making 32

Chapter Three - Habits for Happiness 38
    9 Communication Habits that Save Relationships 39
    All About the 80/20 Rule 45
    Measuring Your Happiness with the Magic Relationship Ratio 45
    Stop Freaking Out About these 6 "Problems" 47

Chapter Four - Love in Every Way 53
    All You Need to Know about Love Languages 53
    How to Use Nonverbal Communication to your Advantage 58
    Less-Known but Powerful Ways to Show Your Partner Love 60

Chapter Five - Decoding Your Partner 66
    Understanding Your Partner's Particular Needs 67
    5 Absolutely Essential Things to Do When Your Partner Has
    Experienced Trauma 72

Chapter Six - It's All About You 77
    How to Instantly Become a Better Partner 78
    Understanding Your Relationship Attachment Style 84
    Must-Know Tips for Starting a New Relationship When You Have a
    History of Bad Relationships 88

Chapter Seven - The Ticking Time Bomb 95
    When to Press the Pause or Stop Button 96
    How to Bring Up Your Concerns the Right Way 100
    5 Statements to Instantly Defuse a Heated Discussion 104
    What NOT to Say During an Argument 106
    9 Relationship Problems You Cannot Fix 108

Chapter Eight - Deepening the Bond 115
    Exercises and Activities that Strengthen Relationships 116
    Bond Instantly with these 8 Fun Couple Activities 123

Conclusion 130

Introduction

Remember the first time you laid eyes on your significant other? It might not have been love at first sight, and maybe not even second sight, but I'm willing to bet on one thing: you thought winning them over would be the biggest challenge. You wanted so badly to get that date and when you finally succeeded in getting it, you wondered what you could do to get them to really like you. Now, months or years down the road, just when you thought it would all be smooth-sailing, you've found the puzzle only gets more confusing. Now, you realize winning them over was the easy part. Coexisting happily? That's a whole different ballpark.

Communication was simple when it was all sweet nothings and getting to know each other. Now that you're closer, there are different things on your mind. You have concerns, you have unmet needs, and you've noticed other ways you'd like to improve your relationship. Chances are that your significant other feels exactly the same way.

The problem is that these concerns are never easy things to express. If done incorrectly, it could hurt your partner's feelings and do irreparable damage. And yet if you don't express yourself, you just might explode, also doing irreparable damage. You're feeling a little cornered, aren't you? I don't blame you.

Your mind is probably swirling with a million questions like, "How can I communicate with my partner in the most effective way possible? How can I go about maintaining my happiness as well as his or her happiness? And how on earth can I do all this without completely exhausting myself?"

Even if you have pretty good communication already, why stop there? Aim for the stars. Your relationship deserves it.

Studies have shown that poor communication is one of the major reasons why a relationship fails. Many of those relationships could have been saved if they had this guide in their lives. A relationship ended over bad communication is a relationship that could have been saved. We can all learn to communicate better, no matter how shy or ineffective we may be now. All we need are the right tools and motivation. The fact you're here now proves there's a high chance you already have the motivation. Good for you. Now all you need is the expert advice. That's where I come in.

I've spent key years of my life studying the way humans interact with each other – how to use each gesture or glance as a key to a person's true feelings and intentions. I've paid close attention to the way individuals communicate and I've unlocked the secrets to what succeeds, and what inevitably fails. By staying attuned to the needs of others, I've discovered little-known tricks that can instantly shift a tense dynamic to an open, loving one. I've gained my expertise by staying aware of what works and what doesn't. I've watched relationships deteriorate over poorly phrased sentences, and I've seen couples reignite their love with just a few words. I've tested my methods on couples on the brink, and I've watched them blossom into their best selves. Even today, couples I've worked with continue to thank me. You see, once you have the tools, you're set for life.

With my help, you and your partner are one-step closer to the fantasy you both share – the one where you can say anything to each other and solve absolutely any problem together. You may not know you share this fantasy, but you do. When communication is strained, both partners desperately wish it could be better. You may think they don't notice, but trust me, they notice as much as you do. With my help, you'll make great communication the new norm. You'll start a brand new chapter where you can look back and think, "I can't believe how far we've come!" This book will strengthen you and your partner as a team. And do you want to know something else? A great team can do absolutely anything together.

Don't let this opportunity for growth pass you by. I've known many couples to express deep regret when they know they didn't try as hard as they could have. They continue to be haunted by times they were offered good advice and they said, "Maybe later." Truth is, the longer you wait to make these changes, the more stuck you become in your old ways. The longer you communicate to your partner in the wrong way (or don't communicate at all), the more hurt and strain your relationship accumulates. How much longer before your love breaks under the weight of it?

Choose love and choose your partner, by saying 'yes' to better relationship communication skills. Your new, happier future together is so close – it starts on the next page! So what are you waiting for?

Chapter One - Relationships 101

If there's one topic that dominates music, literature, film, you name it, it's without a doubt our romantic relationships. Do you ever wonder why this is? Romantic love is certainly not the strongest emotion we feel, and new parents would argue it's not even the strongest form of love. So why then do we continue to write and make art about it? The answer is simple: it's because we still don't understand it.

Romance and relationships are some of the most puzzling aspects of our lives. Feelings of attraction can come on unexpectedly, causing confusion and taking over our rational minds. Sometimes we have these feelings when it makes no sense at all to feel them. Swept up in new, burning romances, people can behave unlike their true selves and lose sight of their better judgment. And when we get into relationships, we enter a whole new realm of emotional confusion.

There's a bit of a paradox, isn't there? We get to know our significant others very well, and at the same time, we become more aware of how much we don't know. They are the people we know best of all, and yet they can also be the biggest mysteries. We may know their emotional responses, their habits, their tics, but rarely do we know *why* they are this way. Better communication is how we eliminate this distance.

Before we dive in, let's take a quick pause and remember something profoundly important: two halves make a whole. For a relationship to succeed, two individuals need to hold up their side of the equation. This doesn't just mean taking turns washing the dishes or splitting the bill. It means doing the self-work to be a better partner. It means reflecting on your needs and wants, your behavior, and considering how to be better when you're confronted with your dysfunctions.

So let's go to step one. Remember when we mentioned reflecting on our needs? Before we can begin to communicate our needs and wants, we must first know what our basic needs are.

The Vital Needs Every Relationship Must Fulfill

As complicated as relationships may seem, our basic needs are fairly easy to categorize. For a relationship to thrive, there are five basic but very important needs that should be met for both partners. Please note these basic needs aren't the only needs we have, they are just the ones we all share. Each individual has unique needs, depending on their personality and background, but for simplicity's sake, we'll start with the basics.

You may encounter certain personalities that have a higher tolerance for the lack of one of these needs. For example, have you ever met a boring couple that seemed just fine, despite their lack of variety? Or a couple that stimulated each other intellectually, but didn't have a true emotional connection? Many couples can make it work without taking care of all five needs. But the big questions remain: are they truly happy? Couldn't they be happier?

The Need to Feel and Be Secure

Without this need, a relationship is nothing. It's the most basic of the five and it refers to our deep need to feel emotionally, physically, and psychologically intact. If your significant other claims this need is not being met, serious work needs to be done. Feeling a lack of security could indicate a few types of problems: our physical well-being is threatened or we are being emotionally abused on some level. It all comes down to one partner feeling hurt and anticipating being hurt again, sometimes going through huge lengths to avoid it.

Many people don't realize this need is unmet because they think abuse is always intentional. This isn't true at all. Many partners don't realize they're using emotionally abusive tactics such as gaslighting or manipulation. They may have these responses wired into their brain without realizing how much damage it does.

When your need to feel secure isn't being met...

You feel like you can't be vulnerable around your partner. You fear they may verbally or physically hurt you if things don't go their way. You worry that instead of being met with love, you'll encounter more pain or distress. You constantly think of how they are going to react in response to something you do or say; this prevents you from expressing what you need to express. You fear that if you're honest about how you feel, you will be dismissed, mocked, or you might incite anger. You get the distinct feeling that if you share your needs, you will receive a negative response.

The Need to Feel Significant

Let's clear up a misconception: security and significance are not the same things. You may have total confidence that your partner won't hurt you, but is this enough to feel valued and special? It shouldn't be. Giving someone security is common decency, but showing them they're significant is a loving act. When our partner makes us feel significant and special, we feel good about ourselves and are overcome with warmth, knowing everything we give them is appreciated. We feel like the love we give is being received, and not just draining through a bottomless pit. This, in turn, encourages us to show even more love.

A person who has been cheated on is an example of someone who has had their need for significance compromised. There's no worse way to show someone they aren't special than by getting involved with another person behind their back.

When we get into a fight, we can continue to show our partners they're special by apologizing when we do something wrong. This shows we considered their feelings, tried to see their point of view, and are trying to make up for our wrongdoing. Show your partner love and appreciation. Otherwise, what's the point?

Make your partner feel significant by showing them love, and responding to their loving gestures with appreciation and affection.

When your need to feel significant isn't being met...

You find yourself worrying about your partner's infidelity or whether they truly love you. You may start to feel disposable, like your partner doesn't really see you for who you are. You don't feel particularly special in your partner's life. You feel like you serve a function, and not much more than that. You find yourself overcome by the feeling that you've given them everything, yet it's still somehow not enough.

The Need for Variety

When we get to know someone extremely well, our lives begin to form a routine. This is a normal occurrence, and unfortunately, the boredom that arises from it is normal too. To keep a relationship healthy and both partners happy, it's vital that we switch things up every once in a while. Studies have shown that we feel closer to our partners when engage in stimulating activities together.

This could mean anything: going out for dinner instead of cooking, signing up for a fun activity instead of staying home, or even doing something new in the bedroom. Whatever is part of your normal routine, do something completely different.

When both partners have busy work or family lives, a routine is inevitable. But it's completely within your power to make sure it doesn't become boring. Reignite the fire by adding a little more adventure!

When your need for variety isn't being met...

You don't feel as excited by your partner as you used to. It feels like you're stuck in a loop. It feels like your life together is just a series of tasks that need to get finished. It's been a while since you experienced a rush or a thrill together. A part of you longs to feel what you felt at the beginning of your relationship.

The Need for Emotional Connection

If a relationship is going to make it long-term, emotional intimacy is profoundly important. To maintain any close relationship in our lives, we need to make time to connect and allow ourselves to relate to each other. Sometimes this can come very easily to two people, but it's also completely normal for some couples to have to try a little harder. This doesn't mean you're any less meant for each other. Cultural, background, or personality differences can all be contributing factors to two people being more reticent. Start by sharing something honest and vulnerable, and invite your partner to share something similar.

When your need for emotional connection isn't being met...

Your partner sometimes seems like a mystery and there are times it feels like you don't really know them. You get the distinct feeling they don't understand you, and you, too, find their actions puzzling and confusing. You spend a lot of time wondering about them and why they do what they do. You may also feel there's something they need to say, but they're resisting saying it. You also feel the urge to share and open up, but there's never quite enough time. It all gets swept up in another moment.

The Need for Personal Expansion

If your relationship ticks the above four boxes, good for you. You've got a good relationship in your life. Want to know how to make it better? Give each other opportunities for expansion. In other words, help each other grow. Personal expansion can come in many forms, but essentially, we satisfy this need by feeling we've learned something or are learning something from one another.

In a healthy relationship, both partners encourage each other to be the best versions of themselves. They do not act complacent about their partner's goals or achievements, and they certainly do not put each other down. Give your partner positive, gentle feedback and constructive criticism.

Another way we fulfill this need is by stimulating our partner intellectually. Get into a discussion and teach each other new things. Expand each others' minds. Believe it or not, this all comes down to our biological need to procreate for further evolution. We want to find a partner we can truly collaborate with; someone who brings evolved qualities to the table or will evolve with us.

When your need for personal expansion isn't being met...

Your partner makes you feel stagnant. Sometimes you even wonder if they're holding you back from what you could truly accomplish. They don't inspire you in any way. When you get into discussions, it doesn't always feel like you're on the same page. You're often bored or confused by what they talk about. You don't think your partner is very wise or very smart.

The Five Stages of a Relationship

After studying hundreds of different couples, well-known relationship coach, Dr. Susan Campbell, noticed something interesting: just like human beings, relationships have their own lifetimes, made of five different stages. Each stage has its own distinct patterns and with a little self-awareness, all couples will be able to identify where exactly their relationship is.

Unlike with human beings, however, each stage will vary in length from couple to couple. And not every couple is lucky enough to learn the lessons of every single stage, especially the hardest stage of them all, Stage Two. To ensure you and your significant other power through these levels with love, trust, and grace, it's best to inform yourself on what they are.

STAGE ONE: Romance & Attraction

Of all the stages, this is the one you likely know most about. Hollywood films have convinced many people that stage one is what relationships are like all the time – but this could not be further from the truth. At this early point in the relationship, both partners are completely infatuated by each other. We still see each other through rose-tinted glasses, only seeing the positive aspects of our partner while in denial about their negative traits. Here, we still don't quite see our partners exactly as they are.

Your five needs are suspended in this stage because we are less likely to notice if they're not being fulfilled. We're more likely to shrug things off and give our partners the benefit of the doubt because the relationship is so new. We are very easily satisfied at this stage, choosing to see what we want to see.

The length of this stage varies wildly. Some couples progress to the next level after as little as two months and for some lucky couples, it can last up to two years – but rarely longer than that. Stage one generally lasts until partners decide to declare some sort of permanence. For some people, this is when they decide to start dating exclusively, and for others, it may be moving in together. How permanence is perceived varies from person to person.

STAGE TWO: Disillusionment & Struggle

After the euphoria and rush of stage one, we progress to the most difficult part of our relationship. This is when the rose-tinted glasses come off for the first time. We finally begin to see our partner and relationship as they are, and disappointment will begin to seep in. One or both partners will begin to long for how things were at the beginning of the relationship. This is where the balancing act comes in: how can we maintain our personal freedom while also being a good partner?

It's important to remember that going through this is completely normal. Because the media has given us such an unrealistic idea of love, we tend to jump to conclusions at the second stage. As soon as we encounter these problems, we think the relationship must be doomed. I'll tell you now: most problems that occur at this stage *can* be fixed!

To progress to the next stage, it's crucial that partners learn to:

- Accept each other for who they are and not who they want them to be.
- Come to an agreement and compromise about the behaviors and habits creating tension in the relationship.
- Acquire tools and strategies for positive self-transformation.
- Communicate honestly, kindly, and constructively.
- Embrace change and stop trying to fight it.

All at once, our needs come into play. If a need isn't being met, this is where we begin to feel that something is wrong. And if we're at all self-aware, we'll know exactly what this need is. Solving unmet needs now is the key to meeting them long-term.

Most divorces and break-ups happen during this period. It can last months or sometimes even years. Couples can be together for a long time and remain stuck in this stage, unhappy until they finally decide to part. Individuals are tested at this stage. How we choose to act and treat each other will determine the course our relationship takes. If we reject the lessons we need to learn, these problems may surface again in the next relationship.

STAGE THREE: Stability & Mutual Respect

If you make it through the storm, congratulations. There's more peace and harmony in stage three. Here, relationships have matured in a big way and both partners, whether they realize it or not, are better versions of themselves. Strategies are used and compromises are respected. Instead of trying desperately to change your partner, you focus on what's in your control. Let's use an example:

At <u>stage two</u>, Sam and Diane were constantly fighting. Diane would come home from work and see him sprawled in front of the sofa, watching violent TV shows and with an array of junk food spread out on the coffee table. This was his after-work routine. Sam wanted to relax and feel at home, but Diane wanted things to be cleaner and more organized. In their fights, Sam called Diane too strict and controlling, and she called him a messy slob.

At stage three, Sam and Diane have accepted each other's different needs. Diane now understands that Sam needs to let loose in order to de-stress from work. Sam also understands that Diane needs to see a clean and quiet environment to de-stress from her own job. The solution? On some nights, Sam can unwind how he wants, but he puts the TV volume lower so Diane can use a meditation app in the next room. Other nights, Diane can read in peace and quiet, while Sam watches his TV shows using headphones in the next room. And on special nights, they'll watch a show they both want to see and get snacks they both enjoy. If anything bothers them, they'll bring it up gently and kindly, without putting the other person down.

In stage three, you've decided to compromise and you are now adjusting to life with these new changes implemented. You are finally beginning to understand what makes a good partner. You no longer see compromises as infringements on your personal freedom, instead, you see them as opportunities for cooperation. All conflicts that arise are dealt with maturely.

The needs for emotional connection and personal growth are likely well-met during this stage. To avoid becoming bored and stagnant, make sure there's a healthy dose of variety.

STAGE FOUR: Love & Commitment

Here, love is fully-formed. All our actions spell out our commitment to our significant other. Not only have you accepted each other and learned to compromise, you've accepted your life together as *your life*. This doesn't always mean marriage, but it is here that two partners are truly ready for marriage. In stage three, we accept our partner's idiosyncrasies, but in stage four, we love and embrace these differences.

Couples will still experience tension and conflict in this stage, but this is usually circumstantial or incited by new life events. Here, they've already worked out a dynamic for the situations they know well, but inevitably, situations they're not prepared for arise.

For example, Sam and Diane no longer get into heated arguments about how to behave at home. However, one evening at a dinner party, Sam told a story about Diane that really embarrassed her. He thought it would be funny but she argued it was too personal. Conflict like this is bound to arise sometimes, but using the tools they've learned in Stage Two, they can come to a resolution.

At this stage, it's important that partners make sure their needs for variety and emotional connection are met. The commitment has been solidified and sometimes this can mean the routine has begun to control their life.

STAGE FIVE: Symbiosis & Sharing

When we reach the final stage of our relationship, we are no longer insular and contained. Here, we begin to work together to give back something to the world. Once a strong foundation has been built, it's natural to want to build upwards and outwards.

This can mean children, but not for every couple. It can also mean starting a project or business. You know a couple is in this stage when they have a giving, almost parental quality to them or they just seem to *get things done* together. It's the opposite of two young lovebirds locking themselves in a room and not talking to anyone; a solid couple wants to share with the world in some form. They are ready to collaborate in every way.

Chapter Two - The Diagnosis

Think of the last time you went to the doctor. It doesn't matter what it was for, whether it was serious or completely mild, every single time you've had to be surveyed for a diagnosis. Before any solutions can be arrived at or any treatment administered, the symptoms must be noted and analyzed. It doesn't matter how potent the medicine is; if it's treating an ailment you don't have, it won't fix what's really wrong with you.

This same principle applies here. You can read up on great relationship advice, but not all of it will be helpful for your specific situation. If you want to improve your relationship, you're going to need to get real about what the issues are. The following chapter will focus on identifying your relationship's problem points. Be honest with yourself. The signs are there, you just need to notice them.

6 Big Signs You and Your Partner Need to Communicate Better

1. **You talk about your partner more than you talk to them**

It's completely normal to discuss our relationship with our friends and family, especially when we need advice, but consider this important question: do you ever share these same issues directly with your partner? How much do your communications *about* your partner outweigh your communications *with* them?

2. **You've become irritable around your partner or vice versa**

At one point in your relationship, it seemed like your partner could do anything and you'd let it blow past you. But now, it takes a lot less for you to lose your patience with them. You find yourself becoming irritated over small things that never used to bother you before. This is a key sign one of your needs is not being met, and a warning sign that you need to open up about it before you snap. Be honest with yourself and consider the real reason behind your lowered tolerance.

3. You find yourself wondering what your partner is truly feeling

We should never feel like our partner is a total mystery. If you frequently find yourself trying to figure out your partner like they're a complicated puzzle, then there's a lot that needs to be cleared up between you two. In a healthy relationship with great communication, we're on the same page as our partners 99% of the time.

4. You and/or your partner are prone to stonewalling

When one partner shuts down, refuses to be vulnerable and cooperate, this is called stonewalling. This goes deeper than the silent treatment. Someone who is stonewalling you will still speak to you, but you'll get the distinct feeling they have their guard up. They're not being real and they may even be playing games. A person who stonewalls is not communicating something that needs to be shared. Why else would they have such a strong reaction to being vulnerable?

5. You avoid certain topics and feel like you're walking on eggshells

Sometimes there is more than one elephant in the room. Sometimes it may even feel more like a mammoth. Does the room feel heavy with words unsaid? Is there noticeable tension? This is a big sign that the relationship is struggling with open communication. For some reason, neither partner is comfortable just saying what needs to be said. And chances are, this isn't the only thing they're struggling to say.

6. One or both partners is being passive-aggressive

Passive-aggression is a big sign that something needs to be said. It occurs when someone does not want to be obnoxious or outright aggressive, so they try to air their grievances without being completely upfront. They're not really being honest, they are trying to talk about it without *really* talking about it. Sarcasm is another form of passive-aggression when it is used in a nasty way. Whenever we can't communicate directly, we find more indirect ways of making our feelings known.

The Reasons Why We Don't Communicate

Knowing the reason behind poor communication won't give us the tools we need, but it'll show us where to begin working. How can we expect to get anywhere if we don't know where to start?

- **One or both partners has trouble being vulnerable**

This is a common reason why people don't communicate and it is an obstacle that can be overcome with practice. There are many extremely valid reasons why someone may have trouble being vulnerable. Sometimes there's a history of abuse, cultural differences, an oppressive upbringing, or maybe it's just that person's personality.

- **You're scared of being criticized**

When we're in a relationship with a highly critical person, this can affect our ability to be open with them. We're less likely to be honest because we'll constantly be thinking about how they'll react to our honest thoughts. Even if it's something that won't upset them at all, we may over-anticipate this reaction out of anxiety. It's important that the critical partner is identified in this scenario.

- **You don't realize there's something you need to say**

Many people in the world have been taught to live with a 'get up and move on' sort of attitude. While this is a great way to approach life's problems, it can cause communication to suffer in a relationship. Why? Because this attitude gets us in the habit of just swallowing our pain and distress, without acknowledging it. We try to suppress these feelings and in doing so, we become less self-aware about how we truly feel. So when there's something we desperately need to bring up with our partner, we may not be aware of what it really is. This can result in a lot of backhanded and passive-aggressive behavior.

- **Your lives have become busy**

When we're busy, we don't just fail to communicate because we literally have less time to talk. Having less time with our partner means we also start to lose a sense of intimacy. They're not around so we are no longer able to feed our connection. When we feel distant from our partners, we are less likely to want to share something personal with them.

- **One of you is keeping a secret**

It's a possibility we don't like to consider, but it remains a potentiality for any couple. When we have something to hide, it can take a toll on communication as a whole. Subconsciously or fully consciously, the partner with the secret starts to keep their distance, knowing that it's the only way they can protect their secret. Often, their significant other will also sense that something is off, which only leads to greater distance and even worse communication. This secret is not always a betrayal like infidelity.

- **You're holding onto resentment**

When one partner is holding onto a grudge, they stop allowing themselves to connect with their significant other. The grudge could be over something silly or something huge, but it always has the same effect. Resentment is so strong it can almost feel like a third entity in the relationship. Even if we verbalize that we've forgiven our partner, as long as there's any ounce of resentment, this forgiveness is not entirely present. When we secretly or not-so-secretly hold a grudge, communication can feel strained or completely nonexistent. The partner on the receiving end will feel like there's a wall they can't get past.

The 10 Communication Mistakes You Don't Know You're Making

Another beginner's step to improving relationship communication is to look at what's impeding progress. Before we can even think about remedies and solutions, we need to identify what behavior absolutely needs to go. It's time to be honest with yourself.

1. You're refusing to be accountable for anything

When we're faced with a situation that distresses us, it's difficult to accept we played a part in making it happen. But the harsh reality is we usually do. When we're in a relationship, it is vital that we learn to take accountability for our part in a situation. Apologies don't mean anything if there isn't accountability to back it up. When we learn to own up to our actions, we create a safe space of honesty, vulnerability, and kindness in our relationship. It reinforces the idea that you're a team. Yes, you both played a part in creating an unfavorable circumstance, but most importantly, you can both work together to prevent it in the future. Don't treat your partner like the villain; treat them like your team member.

2. You're dismissing your partner's feelings

Here's a secret you likely already know: sometimes you're going to think your partner's feelings are ridiculous. Sometimes, you won't understand them at all and you may have the urge to just walk away. It's important to stress, however, that you should *never* walk away or shrug them off. Dismissing your partner's feelings can do a lot of damage. You need to understand that even if it doesn't mean anything to you, it could be causing your partner a lot of pain. When you dismiss your partner's feelings you're telling them you don't care about how they feel. This can create even deeper pain for them and ruin communication in your relationship.

3. You're using harsh or abusive language

You could be saying something completely reasonable, but if you're using abusive language or calling them names to make your point, you're doing yourself and your partner a disservice. When we use abusive language to convey a message, it is far less likely to be heard. No one wants to be scolded like a child or made to feel like a failure. The language and tone we use should encourage our partner to do better, not shame them for what they've done. As soon as we do this, we make it more likely for our partners to act out of fear, instead of empowerment and love. This type of behavior can ruin a relationship and in some cases, it can even traumatize the person on the receiving end. It is essential to fix this behavior as soon as it arises.

4. You're yelling and screaming

If you're raising your voice or yelling at your partner, you're killing all chances of seeing eye-to-eye. Just like using abusive language, this is the wrong way to deliver a message. It doesn't matter how rational that message is or how right you are; when you yell and scream, you make your message less powerful. The delivery of your message should encourage your partner to cooperate with you, not cower in fear. When we act with aggression, we increase the likelihood of our partner's reacting with defensiveness. As soon as we do this, we enter combat mode. Nothing gets solved when we are in combat mode.

5. You always concede and apologize

It's not always about being too aggressive, you can also be too submissive. If you find yourself constantly agreeing and apologizing even though you didn't do anything wrong, you're taking the easy way out. It's true that we should pick our battles and sometimes it's more important to swallow our ego instead of arguing, but this shouldn't be a common occurrence. If you find yourself constantly running into the same problem with your partner, it's time to stop backing down so easily. If you continue to take the blame, the problem will never get solved because you're not the person who's causing it. For the sake of the relationship, you need to tell your partner how they are creating the situation at hand. Help them see the opportunity to make things better.

6. You throw around absolutes

Throwing around words like 'always' or 'never' when you don't mean it literally can sometimes be detrimental to the situation at hand. For example, if you say to your partner, "You're always whining" or "You never help me with anything" this is likely not an accurate statement. If it's not literally true, it can come across as hurtful because you're exaggerating the problem. It's essential that you stick to the facts when you're bringing up a problem, and steer-clear of finger-pointing language.

7. You're being *too* honest

We always hear that we should never keep anything from our partner, but that's not entirely true. It is possible to be *too* honest and it can cause a great deal of damage. As a rule of thumb, it's usually a good idea to be honest about something that you *did,* but it's not always necessary to tell them everything you *think*. If you're planning on having lunch with an ex, you should absolutely be honest about this. But should you tell your partner you find one of their friends attractive? Definitely not. This type of honesty can hurt someone's feelings.

8. You're not allowing yourself to be vulnerable

It's normal to feel some resistance towards being vulnerable. After all, we're giving someone very personal information and it's natural to want to protect ourselves. But for a relationship to be healthy, it's vital that we learn to be vulnerable with our partner. All this means is we need to share how we feel in an honest and open manner. It means showing a side of ourselves that we don't normally show anyone. To truly achieve a sense of intimacy, we need to let people in. Avoid communicating enigmatically or using sarcasm and humor in serious situations.

9. You're expecting your partner to read your mind

This is a common reason why people get mad at each other and it's easily prevented. The frustration stems from the idea that our partners should just *know* when something is wrong, and they should just *know* what to do to fix it. This is not at all fair to your significant other. Of course your emotions and needs seem obvious to you. After all, you're the one feeling them! There are many reasons your partner wouldn't notice and most of them are not worth getting mad over. The fact of the matter is when you're not expecting someone to have a certain reaction, you're less likely to notice the signs. So give your partner a break and just be honest. Once you get the problem out of the way, you can start working on solutions.

10. You attack your partner and not the issue

When our significant others do something that bothers us, it can be tempting to start attacking their character, but we should never do this. Let's say they completely forgot to pick up groceries on the way home from work. As maddening as this can be, do not say, "You're so forgetful. You forget everything!" Even if they do have a tendency to forget, always focus on the issue at hand. Instead of calling them forgetful, bring up what's really inciting your anger in this specific situation, i.e. forgetting the groceries. Consider saying something like, "I really wish you'd try harder to remember these important errands. I would feel much better if we could share the task of picking up groceries." You could even offer a solution like creating a phone reminder. You could also take some accountability and add, "I should have texted you to remind you. I know you have a lot on your mind after work." When we attack our partner's character, this is a put-down. It can make them feel terrible about themselves and this isn't helpful in creating a solution.

How many of these problems and signs have you recognized in your relationship? The more that you resonate with, the more desperately your relationship needs better communication. And don't worry, most of this is completely fixable!

Chapter Three - Habits for Happiness

The power of baby steps is highly underrated. Just think about it – our lives are not made of big achievements and end-destinations. It's made of the smaller struggles, the day-to-day grind, and the little victories that accumulate into big victories.

One of the major ways we set ourselves up for failure is by focusing on the end result and not the small steps that get us there. For example, we may say we want to lose weight, but instead of creating achievable step-by-step goals like "Only have dessert once a week" or "Eat one salad every day," we'll create big goals like "Lose 5 lbs in one week" without a single method to help our progress.

The secret to achieving anything is this: create good habits that support your goal. Want fantastic communication in your relationship? It's probably not going to be excellent immediately. And progress will be slow if you don't plan smaller, achievable steps. If you want better communication, you'll need to create better communication habits. It starts with implementing one technique, then another, and learning to make these new tools part of your routine. To succeed, you need to reinvent your norms.

9 Communication Habits that Save Relationships

1. Check-in with each other every day

This act is so simple, yet so powerful. At least once per day, get an update on how your partner is doing. This doesn't always mean asking "How are you?" it can also mean asking how their day was when you see each other after work. If you remember your partner mentioning a difficult upcoming meeting, ask how that meeting went. By doing this, we show our significant other we care and that we are listening.

2. Learn to use "I feel/It feels" statements

When you start a statement with "I feel" it turns a potentially accusatory or assumptive statement into something more gentle. For the best possible outcome in any situation, especially when one partner is in a tender state, "I feel" statements are the best way to communicate with them. Notice the difference between these two statements:

- "You're not listening to me. You haven't heard anything I've said."
- "I feel like you're not listening to me. It feels like you haven't heard anything I've said."

Switch the emphasis from "you" to "I." Notice how this makes something that could be interpreted as accusatory or aggressive suddenly becomes an honest observation. You're not telling your partner how they acted; you are emphasizing how you are experiencing their actions. There's a big difference. This is harder to argue with because when we explain how we feel, we become vulnerable. Since we are just saying "it feels" that way, we give our partner the opportunity to say that's not what they meant. When we don't use "it feels," we corner our partner, making their cooperation less likely.

3. Reconsider what you deem 'unimportant'

This less-known tip is remarkably effective at transforming relationships. When our partner says something we don't think is that important, we fail to make one massive realization: it could be very important to them! Whenever you're about to say "That's nice, honey" or perhaps even ignoring what they say altogether, consider the positive impact a proper response would have. If your partner just got home from work and she mentions in passing that she made a new friend, do not just nod and say "Oh, cool." Say enthusiastically, "That's wonderful you made a new friend."

Want to know something else? If your partner shows enthusiasm, even if it's for something small, you must meet that enthusiasm with interest or at the very least, you must acknowledge it properly. If you're taking a walk and your partner says, "Oh look! What a pretty bird!" it's very likely that you don't really care about the pretty bird. But you should still never ignore your partner when they are excited about something. Say "I wonder what kind of bird that is" or just agree with them by saying, "That is a very pretty bird, indeed." You should respond at least once to their statement.

All of this creates a closer connection and allows your partner to feel truly significant. It diminishes feelings of being ignored and unnoticed. If your partner's need for significance is not being met, this is a habit you should implement into your daily communication.

4. Ask them questions about their interests

Get in the habit of asking your partner about topics or events that interest them. I don't just mean subjects that they sort-of think are interesting, but the topics that get them really excited, even if they're a little silly. If your partner is into celebrity gossip, ask them what their favorite celebrity is up to lately, or ask what they thought of the latest article about them.

Think of the last time you saw your partner's eyes light up when they were talking. That's a good place to start. When we get into the habit of doing this, we build a stronger connection with our partners. It makes them feel special because you not only remember what they love, but you care enough to let them talk about it. As they speak, show genuine enthusiasm for what they're saying.

5. Say at least one positive or encouraging thing to your partner every day

It doesn't have to be a long, drawn-out love letter; just say at least one positive thing to your partner daily, even if it's short and sweet. It can be anything, and it should be spoken with enthusiasm. You're also free to do this by text. Some ideas are:

- "You've been working so hard lately. You know, I really admire what a hard-worker you are."
- "I know you've been stressed out, but I think you're handling everything very well."
- "You look wonderful today."

If you can't think of anything, then why not a simple but heartfelt "I love you"? Pepper more positive statements into your daily communication with your partner and you'll find your entire dynamic instantly becomes more loving.

6. If you disagree, gently invite them to reflect

You can't avoid disagreements with your partner, but you *can* avoid turning them into full-blown arguments. Instead of "you should" or "you shouldn't" statements, encourage them to reflect. Don't push an idea on them, lead them to it.

Let's use an example. Kelly has planned a lunch date with a friend that has always put her down and been mean to her. Her partner, James, doesn't think it's a good idea for them to meet up. Instead of saying, "You shouldn't meet up with her," he chooses to incite reflection. He asks, "Do you think she'll behave the same way she did last time?" and "What do you think will be different this time?" James allows his opinion to be known by using "I" statements. He says, "I just worry that she'll be a bad friend, like she normally is. I don't like to see you upset."

Use questions to invite your partner to reflect, and if you must add your opinion, always use "I" statements.

7. Still say 'please' and 'thank you'

When we stop using our basic manners with someone, it's a troubling sign that we've started to take them for granted. Make sure that no matter what happens you are always in the habit of saying 'please' and 'thank you' at the appropriate moments. Even if you're in a bad mood, you should still say it. This is the most basic way to show appreciation for someone, and when we stop, we display a sense of entitlement. You may think your partner won't notice but they will, especially when they've put considerable effort into providing you with something. Always show appreciation for your partner's efforts and adhere to these basic good manners.

8. Engage in pillow talk

Even when both partners have busy schedules, there's no reason they can't enjoy a little pillow talk. After all, we all need to go to bed at some point! Pillow talk occurs at the end of the day, when couples are winding down in bed. It consists of intimate and relaxed conversation where both partners can share their thoughts. Couples can choose to cuddle or not, but physical contact tends to create a more loving atmosphere. If you're having a somewhat tense conversation, cuddling can reduce combativeness and increase the likelihood of cooperation. When couples get in the habit of engaging in pillow talk, they have a greater chance at keeping the intimacy and connection alive in their relationship.

9. Share openly with your partner

To create a greater sense of intimacy and connection, don't wait to be asked questions – just start sharing interesting parts of your day. Tell them about funny things that happened at work, or about that hilarious text your friend sent you. If you're upset by something that happened, be vulnerable and share it with them. Once you start doing this you create an environment where sharing and openness is not just welcome, but completely normal. This means your partner is more likely to share with you as well. When distance grows between two people, they tend to overthink how to make it better. The solution is simple: just start acting like there's no distance at all.

When you share openly with your partner, make sure there's an opening for them to share as well. Do not spend hours talking about just you and your day. Invite them to share things that are exciting or interesting in their life. Of course, some of us are naturally more talkative, and at times, we just can't help it. To ensure that there's an even exchange of conversation, consider the following technique:

All About the 80/20 Rule

If you normally do most of the talking or you sense your partner needs to get something off their chest, opt for the 80/20 rule. This technique is extremely easy and straightforward. When you're talking to your partner, aim to listen 80% of the time and only talk 20% of the time. Don't use this technique in every conversation with your partner, as it's not always appropriate and sometimes it's best to keep it at 50/50. Bring it into play only if your partner needs to express something, if you sense an argument coming on, or if you just want to practice being a better listener.

Measuring Your Happiness with the Magic Relationship Ratio

To better understand relationship happiness, psychologists studied a wide variety of couples by asking them to solve a conflict in 15 minutes. These conversations were taped and watched back nine years later. The same psychologists made predictions about which couples would stay together and which would divorce. Amazingly, a follow-up with the couples involved found that the psychologists were 90% accurate about their predictions!

This led them to their discovery of the Magic Ratio in relationships. They found the major difference between unhappy and happy couples involved the balance of positive and negative interactions during moments of conflict. In this case, a balance of these interactions is not an even split. The Magic Ratio is, in fact, 5:1.

What this means is that for every negative interaction, a healthy and happy couple will have five or more positive interactions to offset the negativity. Negative interactions can include things like eye-rolling, dismissiveness, defensiveness or criticism. And to counteract this, couples should engage in positive interactions like physical affection, well-meaning jokes, apologies, showing appreciation, asking well-intended questions, acceptance, and finding opportunities for agreement. The 5:1 ratio indicates that a couple is happy, healthy, and likely to stay together in the long-run, while a 1:1 ratio is common for couples that are already on the brink of divorce or a break-up.

If there's anything to take away from this ratio, it's that negativity does a great deal of damage! After all, it takes five whole positive interactions just to offset a single negative one. Always keep that in mind moving forward and take care to not let too much negativity seep into your everyday interactions.

Think about the last time you were in conflict with your partner. How many instances of positivity and negativity did you both display?

Stop Freaking Out About these 6 "Problems"

When we get into a deep relationship, so much begins to change – naturally, this makes us worry. Sparks and butterflies are replaced by other feelings, and it isn't entirely clear if this is a good or bad thing. Does this mean you're no longer in love? Is your relationship doomed to fail? Stop worrying! More often than not, couples worry about something that is completely normal.

It's important that we eliminate the habit of freaking out. When we freak out, we are so caught up in the emotion that we don't consider an actual solution. And let me tell you, there *are* solutions. Here are some of the most common relationship problems and better yet, how you can fix them through communication.

1. **Your relationship isn't as exciting as it used to be**

Of all complaints and worries, this one is by far the most common. Ask every single long-term couple and they'll tell you the excitement from their early days has settled. The rush of a new experience has been replaced by a sense of familiarity and closeness. Don't freak out about this! You've found stability.

Don't think of it as having lost something, but as entering a new phase. Your relationship has leveled up.

It's important to distinguish between a relationship that feels less exciting and one that has lost *all* excitement. If you're in the second camp, you've got a little more thinking to do. Either you and your partner have sunk too deep into a rigid routine, or you've lost feelings for one another. Chances are, it's just routine. You've stopped taking care of each others' needs for variety, emotional connection, and personal expansion. Consider having a heart-to-heart and scheduling a date night. Make the effort to spice up your routine. It's not as difficult as you think!

2. Sometimes you desperately want alone time

It's not just normal to want alone time, it's actually very healthy. It means you and your partner have avoided becoming codependent and this is vital for the health of a relationship. Craving solitude means you still value your independence and this is something to feel proud of, not worried about.

Telling your partner you need some time apart shouldn't be a difficult discussion. Be direct, be casual, and avoid turning it into a serious talk – making it seem overly serious will cause your partner to think they did something wrong. Just say, "I haven't had any time to myself in a while and I've always needed solitude to recharge. Can I see you after the weekend is over?" If your partner is less independent than you are, conclude with a plan for your next meeting, so they have something to look forward to. Learning to ask for time alone is a fantastic habit to pick up when you're entering a relationship. Ideally, both partners should be able to take time apart whenever they need, without worrying about the other person.

3. **You caught your partner checking out someone else**

The first time you catch your partner's eyes wandering elsewhere, it can be very distressing. It's okay to be taken aback, but you should realize this is a completely normal occurrence. Even the most committed partners will find other people attractive. Attraction towards other people says nothing about their feelings towards you. Think of the last time you saw someone you found attractive. It could have been someone who passed you on the street, or perhaps it was an attractive celebrity in a movie. Remember how your eyes were drawn to that person? It was automatic, but not fueled by any real emotion. Our brains are wired to enjoy looking at what we find attractive, but eye-candy is all it is unless we chase it.

If this is a rare occurrence, it's probably not worth bringing up with your partner. This will only make them feel embarrassed and awkward. It may even cause them to feel anxious if they are around someone they find attractive – leading to even more discomfort for everyone! I only recommend bringing it up if your partner does it continuously and in an overt or disrespectful way. If their eyes linger too long, or it causes them to stop paying attention to you, feel free to say, "Could you please not do that? It really bothers me." Be direct and clear. And remember, this is a very common problem.

4. You have very different interests

Ask every relationship or marriage coach, and they'll tell you there are some very healthy, happy couples with completely different interests. Sometimes even opposite interests. In some ways, this can be good for a couple. With different interests, it becomes easy to maintain your independence, something that is very good for long-term partners. When a couple has everything in common, they risk spending too much time together, becoming codependent and if they aren't careful, burning out the fire of their relationship. Embrace the fact that you have different interests. Reframe your perspective: you're not too different, you *complement* each other.

If having different interests means you rarely see each other, make sure to schedule at least two days a week where you can partake in the same activity. For example, you could watch a movie at home, go to the cinema, go out to a jazz bar, or a theater performance. You could even choose to learn a new skill together, like pottery or painting. Talk to each other and come to an agreement about a way you can both have fun together.

5. Sometimes your partner really annoys you

You know those moments, don't you? You look over at your partner and you wish they'd just shut up. Or you wish they'd just sit still and stop doing what they're doing. On bad days, you might even become irritated by silly things like how loud they're breathing or how they talk.

Believe it or not, this is normal too – as long as it's not persistent. If you find yourself feeling this way for days on end, there's a chance you've either lost feelings for this person or you're spending too much time together. But if it lasts for only a few or several hours, and then you find yourself returning to your feelings of affection, then you have nothing to worry about. You're just in a normal, long-term relationship! During your moments of annoyance, know that it's normal, and resist the urge to say something hurtful.

6. You don't have sex as much as you used to

Surveys have shown this worry as being one of the most common. Couples, at nearly every stage, have some level of concern that they aren't having sex as much as they should. Truth is, it's completely normal for sex to become less frequent over time. And it's normal for the frequency of sex to fluctuate, depending on what's happening in each person's life. Once the honeymoon phase is over, a relationship begins to settle, and that's totally okay! This does not mean your partner no longer desires you, and it certainly does not mean feelings have been lost. If you're still worried, then schedule a time when you and your partner can drop everything and focus on getting intimate. And try something new you haven't done before!

Chapter Four - Love in Every Way

Communication isn't just about what we say in words. Consider the words, "Oh sure, that would be lovely." You can say that with kindness, but you can also say it with sarcasm, or hesitance. The meaning of everything we say can change based on our tone of voice, facial expression, and the pacing of our speech. Everything we do communicates a message.

Whether we're conscious of it or not, our partner is picking up signals from the way we carry ourselves around them. If you're talking to them but keeping your eyes fixed to your phone, this tells them you're not really interested in the conversation. If your words ask them to open up, but your body is turned towards the TV, this makes your words seem insincere. If you're actively trying to be a better communicator, you must make sure everything you're doing matches the message you're trying to send.

In this chapter, we'll focus on the many ways we can show our partners love. I advise embracing as many expressions of love as you can. And you may be surprised what your partner responds most positively to.

All You Need to Know about Love Languages

Does it sometimes feel like you and your partner are speaking completely different languages? You just might be. Since renowned marriage counselor, Dr. Gary Chapman, identified the five major love languages, it changed the game for millions of relationships. It demystified relationship dynamics, communication, and overall, fueled a greater understanding between partners.

Every single person gives and receives love in a different way. How we do this determines the actions we find loving and the actions we use to express our love for someone else. The way that we naturally communicate love is called our love language. It's common to have more than one, but rarely do we have more than two dominant love languages.

Two partners who are unaware they have different love languages may feel totally confused by one another. They might even feel unloved and unappreciated, unsure of why their attempts to show love have gone unnoticed. To create a smooth exchange of love and appreciation, it is absolutely vital that couples understand their significant other's love language.

Verbal Affirmation

One of the most common love languages is verbal affirmation. This means we use our words to express love and appreciation. People with this love language feel the most loved when someone verbalizes their feelings, pays them compliments, and gives them lots of verbal encouragement. Here are some examples of verbal affirmation:

- If your partner is ready and noticeably trying to look good, say, "Wow, you look fantastic. You're irresistible in this dress."
- If it's a cozy night in and your partner chooses a great movie to watch, say, "You always know just the right movie to pick. You have great taste."
- If your partner does something considerate, say, "This is so wonderful of you. Thank you. I really appreciate that you went through all this trouble for me."

If this is your partner's love language, pay attention to what they say in words. Do not disregard the kind and loving things they say, as this is how they are expressing love for you. Respond to these loving remarks with verbal appreciation.

Quality Time

Another way we communicate love is by giving our loved ones our undivided attention. Those with this primary love language need to feel a sense of togetherness and intimacy. They feel most loved when their partners make time especially for them and give them their complete focus. This isn't just about sitting together and watching a Netflix show, this is about bonding. Vulnerability is a huge plus for people with this love language. Your actions should send the message: "This time is just for you and I. Right now, I want nothing more than to feel close to you."

To communicate love through quality time, all you need to do is schedule a block of time where you can devote all your attention to your partner, and nothing or no one else. This could be a day at the amusement park, a special date night, or a getaway to a romantic place. It could even be as simple as staying in and sharing your days with each other over their favorite wine. Whatever you do, pay attention and listen carefully.

Physical Touch

If you're a very physically affectionate person, it's possible that you prefer to give and receive love through physical touch. A lot can be expressed in the way we touch someone. And as humans, we are wired to respond positively to it. If your partner's love language is physical touch, get used to making loving physical contact. To make your partner feel loved, make sure you hold hands, cuddle, kiss, hug, and nuzzle. People with this love language may also enjoy more sexual intercourse than other people, but this is not always the case.

The best part about this love language is that physical contact is so easy. You don't need much creativity or thought to communicate through touch. When you're passing through the room they're in, give them a peck on the cheek or rub their arm gently. When greeting them or saying goodbye, give them a warm embrace.

Acts of Service

If actions mean everything to you, it's possible you receive and give love through acts of service. When this is your love language, you feel most loved when your partner does something you want them to do. This is not at all about being a slave to your partner's every whim, it's about being thoughtful and doing something they didn't ask you to do. If this is your partner's love language, you should take some time to really think about what they'd appreciate the most. Make some aspect of their day easier on them. For example, you could cook your partner a meal they enjoy or fix one of their broken belongings. It could even be as simple as plugging in their phone if you see the battery is low. Perform actions that actively take care of your partner.

Gift Giving

If your love language is gift-giving, this doesn't mean you're a materialistic person. A gift is just physical proof that you've been thinking about someone. It doesn't need to be fancy or expensive. In fact, it doesn't need to cost anything at all. It's just about putting your loving thoughts and intentions into securing a physical object. It's not about the gift itself, it's about the thought behind it. Get used to giving gifts if this is your partner's love language. If they love chocolate, get a box or bar on your way home from work. If their favorite flowers are in bloom, pick up just one or a whole bouquet. And make sure to treat gift-giving holidays seriously!

How to Use Nonverbal Communication to your Advantage

As we established earlier on in the chapter, your partner is paying attention to everything you're saying, even the things you're not saying in words. To get the best outcome from a conversation, or to soothe them when they are feeling tender, follow these simple but effective nonverbal techniques:

- **Touch your partner in a supportive way**

Don't underestimate the power of touch. Putting an arm around your partner or holding their hand while they talk can make them feel much more at ease. A common tactic couples use when trying to come to an agreement is to cuddle or hold each other in some way, as they talk. Affection and touch can make individuals much more likely to cooperate with each other. Please note, however, that you shouldn't touch your partner if they are extremely angry with you – this can come across as inappropriate and make the situation worse.

- **Keep your facial expression neutral or sympathetic**

When you're listening to your partner speak, make sure your facial expression doesn't discourage them from speaking. If you're in a good mood, keep it sympathetic, and if you're not in a good mood, just keep it neutral. Even if we're upset with our partners, it's important that they feel they can speak without being judged. We may not be saying harsh words, but our facial expressions can still communicate an upsetting message.

Consider this scenario as an example: you're sitting with your partner, explaining to them how you feel very ignored when they're constantly on the phone during your date nights. How would you feel if your partner started looking at you with a raised eyebrow? What if they started scowling? What if it looked like they were about to laugh? Chances are you wouldn't want to continue sharing. And there's even a high likelihood you'd start to feel hesitant about sharing in the future. See? Even when we're not speaking, we're sending a message. Soften your features for a better response.

- **Turn your body towards your partner**

When you're speaking to your partner, especially about something serious, don't simply glance sideways at them. Make sure your entire body is angled towards them. When our bodies are turned away from the person we're speaking to, we send the message that we're not really interested in the conversation at hand. We show we're not truly invested. If your partner is upset or you sense they need some TLC, use your body to face them squarely.

- **Adjust the tone and sound of your voice**

It's not always about what you say, it's also about how you say it. Consider, in the moment, what your partner most needs from you. Do they need to just listen and empathize? If so, speak in a softer, more gentle voice. Do they need reassurance? If so, then speak with a firm, confident voice to make them feel secure. To soothe your significant other, speak slowly as a fast voice can come across as being dismissive.

Less-Known but Powerful Ways to Show Your Partner Love

Showing our significant other love in one or two forms just won't cut it. Why stop there? Whenever you get the chance, take the opportunity to shower them in warmth and positivity. This isn't just limited to the methods I've listed so far. The ways we can engage in loving behavior are endless.

1. Publicly declare how proud you are of them

It doesn't matter who you say it to; when an appropriate time comes up, why don't you proudly share one of your partner's achievements? It doesn't have to be a huge accomplishment, it can be anything that they worked hard on. Recognize your partner's efforts and share their achievement with an outside party. Everyone is taught to stay humble and never brag about their successes, but sometimes we secretly want people to know we succeeded at something. Be the first to share something amazing your partner did. It'll make them feel extremely loved, supported, and they'll likely feel encouraged to keep making progress. This tactic might make them blush at first, but once the shyness wears off, they'll feel very touched.

2. Stand up for your significant other

If something unfair happens to your partner, don't be afraid of speaking up. This doesn't mean you should start a fight or say something nasty, it simply means you should vocalize your support during a difficult situation. Use your common sense to determine the right way to do this. If you're in a conversation with lots of people and someone puts your partner down, counter it by acting as their cheerleader.

Consider this example: Adam and Vanessa are out with a group of friends. Someone starts making fun of Vanessa because she mentioned she was writing a novel. The rude person remarks on how everyone else is working a high-paying corporate job while Vanessa is at home writing stories. Adam doesn't need to start a fight to stand up for her. All he says is, "Writing a novel takes a lot of patience and determination. Vanessa has been working very hard and I think it's wonderful that she's chasing her passion instead of becoming money-obsessed." No negativity required!

3. Make an effort to bond with the people close to them

It's true what they say; when you start dating someone, you date their close friends and family as well. Whether you like it or not, these people are here to stay. And if you don't make the effort to leave a positive impression, their opinions could have an influence on the course of your relationship. When you get to know your partner's close connections, you send the message that you really want to be a part of your loved one's life. You demonstrate you're serious, and you display genuine love. Why? Because you're engaging in an entirely unselfish pursuit. After all, your partner's friends and family don't satisfy any of your needs and desires. Don't give in to the idea that they aren't important because they're not your partner. How you treat them speaks volumes about how you see your relationship.

4. Ask your partner what they enjoy in the bedroom

There's this unhealthy idea that we should all just *know* what our partners want, without ever asking them. Many people are under the mistaken impression that if we can't just figure it out on our own, we're not good in bed. This is a ridiculous notion. We're not mind-readers and every single person has different preferences. A lot of people are not forthcoming about what they like because they don't want to seem demanding, so why not just ask? How can we get it right if we never know?

Even if you already know what your partner likes, there's nothing wrong with having a check-in. Ask them if there's anything you did recently that they enjoyed, and ask them if there's anything you can do better. Learning to communicate openly about sex is one of the best things we can do in our relationships. It also shows our partner how devoted we are to making them happy and meeting their needs. Even if we don't always get it right, it can make the difference to know we're trying.

5. Learn more about a topic that interests them

If your partner is a huge science-fiction nerd, try and watch their favorite show or movie. If they love discussing politics but you don't understand it, ask them to explain something to you. Open up and expand your horizons! Show your partner you're really interested in what they care about. You never know, you may even find that you're interested in it as well. We should always try to create opportunities for bonding with our partner. By engaging with what interests them, we create more intimate moments. This is a sure way to strengthen your connection.

6. Take care of them when they're sick

It's fairly common for women to take on a nurturing role when their partners are sick, but unfortunately it's less common to see it happen the other way around. One of the most loving things we can do for our partners is to take care of them when they're at their weakest. This includes all types of physical and mental ailments, including sickness, depression, or even grief. This doesn't mean we have to wait on them hand and foot; it just means offering some strength when they need it the most. This loving gesture tells our partner that we care for them, even when they are too weak to offer us anything in return.

7. Make time to relive your love story

Every single couple has a unique love story. It encompasses all the wonderful, exciting things about a new romance: how you met, what you first thought of each other, when you knew you wanted to be with them, and so much more. A great way to continue reigniting love and passion is by actively reliving your love story with your partner. Why not revisit the place you had your first date? Or the place you had your first kiss? Or how about just tell each other your different sides of the story? When did you both know it was love? When a couple does this, they're taking a step back to remember why they're with each other. They are disconnecting from their current troubles and making the effort to not lose sight of the magic. We all have a love story; take the time to remember yours.

8. Make plans for the future

Alright, calm down, this doesn't mean you need to start planning your wedding or naming your future children. It just means you need to paint a future with your partner in it. It's not about committing to forever, it's about coming up with shared goals and creating shared dreams. Identify something you can both work towards achieving together. This creates a more hopeful and collaborative environment in the relationship. By doing this, we show our partner that they, too, are part of the dream and part of the goal. It is the positive kind of self-fulfilling prophecy, where we subconsciously do our best to thrive alongside our partner because we have a goal to reach for.

Chapter Five - Decoding Your Partner

In the early days of a romance, getting to know the person you're madly attracted to is an exciting pursuit. Everything about them is fascinating and almost spellbinding. Every new quirk you discover is adorable, even the objectively annoying ones. Their unique qualities draw you in and you're convinced there's no one like them in the world. Your feelings are on fire in the best way possible. You can't wait to fully unravel your partner and deeply get to know them in every single way.

Once things become serious, your attitude is likely to see a shift. This isn't a bad thing. In fact, it's extremely normal, as I've demonstrated in the first chapter. While you still love your partner and their unique quirks, you've also discovered the other dimensions to their personality, the sides that weren't apparent in the early days at all. Every person has a dark side. We all have inner conflicts, our own particular needs, and even when all our secrets are laid bare, there are bad days where we suddenly play to an entirely different tune. Like I mentioned, this is completely normal. This is human nature. This will happen in every relationship you encounter and to be a good partner, you need to learn to roll with it.

Your significant other may feel like a mystery at times, but he or she is far more simple than you think. It all comes down to the basic needs which we all share, and some unique needs which are entirely their own. You'll learn about them over time and gradually perfect how to take care of them. The process of decoding your partner takes awareness, understanding, and kindness, but it's one of the best things you can do for your relationship. This is what love is all about.

Understanding Your Partner's Particular Needs

With every single partner you're with, you're going to need to take the temperature on their various needs. Trouble is, 'needs' is such a vague term, and you may not be sure where to begin. If you want to make your partner happy, consider these different types of needs and make sure you understand your partner's preferences. This may take some intent observation, but you should also feel free to just openly discuss these topics with your partner. This way, there is no confusion at all.

- **Their sex drive and sexual needs**

It's true that our sex drives can fluctuate but some people just have a much higher sex drive than others, at all times. And there are also other people that just don't crave it as much. Assess your partner's needs or just straight-up ask your partner how high they would rate their sex drive. You may find they have a similar sex drive to you, but you may also find you have differing needs. This means that later on you'll need to find a compromise so neither partner feels unsatisfied. You'll also need to discover what they specifically enjoy in the bedroom. Keep in mind that everyone's different and it may even be beneficial to just outright ask your partner what they like.

- **The way they destress and relax**

There are certainly common threads, but for the most part, we all have different ways of destressing and unwinding. For some people, this can mean total peace and quiet, eating healthy food, and taking a walk in the park. At the opposite extreme, some people like watching loud TV, playing video games, and want nothing more than to gorge on greasy pizza. You'll even find that some people like to be social when they relax, and others like to be completely alone. It's always best to find out what your partner's needs are after a long day. Once you know, you can help create the right environment for them when you know they need it the most. It's also perfectly normal for people to have a few ways they like to destress, but you'll likely notice a pattern. If you and your partner have conflicting ways of destressing, make sure to find a way to compromise.

- **Their idea of adventure**

Adventure doesn't always mean skydiving or roller-coasters; our need for adventure arises when we have energy and are in the mood to do something fun. Maybe even something different from our usual routine. We're ready to exert energy, instead of trying to preserve it. A common idea of adventure in the modern day is going out for a night on the town, dancing, and having some delicious cocktails. But some people, even on their best days, don't want to do this at all. Some people like to be indoors and engaging in private activities. Perhaps, they want to cook or bake, or do a home work-out video. When it comes to adventure, we're much more likely to have many ideas of fun. In this case, it's best to note what your partner's favorite thing is, and to rule out what they definitely *do not* consider fun. It's important that whatever they like to do, you either learn to enjoy it too or just accept that they enjoy doing it.

- **Their needs for mental and intellectual stimulation**

To put it simply, what we find mentally and intellectually stimulating is what we find interesting. It encompasses all the topics that we enjoy feeling challenged by and exploring. This is one of the easiest needs to discover as people are more upfront about what mentally stimulates them. You just need to pay attention.

Some people choose to not classify this as a need, but I would beg to differ. When we are deprived of what we find interesting, our personalities wilt and we feel lackluster, perhaps even depressed. Those who stop engaging with topics they enjoy can even complain of feeling less like themselves.

It's important, once we identify these stimulation needs in our partner, to always actively listen and participate as much as we can. What are the topics that bring your partner joy? When do you see their eyes come alive? Whatever these topics are, we must always allow our partner to bring them into the wider conversation. This is how we can help satisfy their need for personal expansion.

- **Their emotional support needs**

Inevitably, a time will arise when your partner needs emotional support. While their needs will vary with each circumstance, you'll notice there are patterns in what they find soothing during times of emotional hardship. For some people, it's important to cry, in which case you should make sure to be an understanding shoulder to cry on. Some people become more hungry and have more cravings during times of emotional stress, in which case, you should try to give them whatever food they find nourishing. There are even people who need to be completely alone to feel supported. They may just want to escape into nature by themselves and they'll need you to understand that. Whenever your partner is going through a time of hurt, try to learn what eases the pain. During these periods, it can also be a good idea to turn to the five love languages.

- **Their spiritual or religious needs**

If your partner doesn't adhere to any specific spiritual or religious practice, then there's no need to worry about this section. However, more often than not, we encounter people that have some shred of spirituality in their lives. Spirituality and religion is a highly personal matter, and it's highly important that we respect our partner's choices and beliefs. Even if it seems silly to us, it brings our partner peace and this is all that matters. Know what your partner's spiritual practices are, when they need to do it, and if there are any other requirements they need to abide by, such as dietary restrictions. We should never argue with their spiritual needs and we should never make fun of them.

- **Their insecurities and needs for reassurance**

You're never going to find a partner without any insecurities. That's just how it is. We're all human and we all have fears shaped by our backgrounds or personalities. It is absolutely vital that you understand what your partner's insecurities are. And most importantly, you must know how to prevent bringing those insecurities to the surface, and what they need from you when they do arise. For example, let's say your partner is insecure about his or her weight. This insecurity might be triggered when they meet someone very thin and attractive. These situations are unavoidable so it's best to come up with an action-plan for when it does happen. Perhaps, later on, you should try and tell your partner how sexy they are, and focus all your energy on making them feel attractive. Or perhaps, your partner would prefer to just forget it and do something that takes their mind off their body entirely. These needs will differ from person-to-person.

5 Absolutely Essential Things to Do When Your Partner Has Experienced Trauma

When you finally meet the person you want to be with, chances are they saw a heck of a lot before you came along. Sometimes even, a little too much. If your partner has been touched by trauma in their romantic or sexual encounters, you'll have to be more gentle with them. This is a non-negotiable. If we don't adjust our behavior, we will never make our partners happy, and we may end up causing more damage.

There are many types of trauma that can leave a painful and emotional scar, from cheating to emotional abuse, and in some cases, more physical kinds of abuse. Communication tactics should always be softened during specific scenarios to ensure you don't trigger them or cause them to withdraw. Always keep the following tips in mind if your partner has endured trauma:

1. **Learn about the trauma in a non-intrusive manner**

Before we know what to do, we must know what we are dealing with. The first step is to try and learn about the traumatic incident. Depending on the severity of the trauma, it may not be as simple as asking our partner what happened. If it is too painful to recount or they are just not ready to tell us, there are only two things we can do: wait for them to feel ready, or ask someone they are close to. A good first action is to tell your partner, "You don't have to tell me anything you don't want to, but I'm always here if you want to share. I just want to know how I can support you in the best way possible." Let them know you care about their past, are ready to listen, but that you won't push them to do anything they don't want to do. It's important that you never force or guilt-trip them in this situation.

2. Consider the types of behavior that may trigger their traumatic memories

This stage requires your deep thought. Think of the qualities and behavior that hurt them during this traumatic incident. Sometimes it's straightforward, such as physical violence, but not all the time. If your partner was cheated on, they may feel triggered by something as mild as you talking to members of the opposite sex. They may become anxious on the nights you go out drinking with your friends. If there are moments where you stop communicating, this could be especially hard for them as they might suspect you are keeping a secret. Identify the behavior involved in the traumatic incident, but also what may have led to it.

3. Decide on alternative or modified ways of behaving

It's not always realistic to eliminate every single behavior that could possibly trigger our partner. While it's easy (and absolutely necessary) to not abuse someone, it's not easy or realistic to completely stop talking to members of the opposite sex. So what can we do instead? It's simple: we must modify the way we engage in this behavior. For example, if you're texting a member of the opposite sex, you could consider letting your partner see the messages so they can ease their worries. If they become anxious when you're out drinking with buddies, consider having a check-in via phone call every couple of hours. Or send them a photo of you at your current location. Get creative about how you can modify your behavior without eliminating completely normal actions. And you should always feel free to simply ask your partner, "What can I do to make you feel better in this situation?"

4. Understand what they need if they are triggered

Hopefully this never happens, but if your partner's trauma is linked to common events, it may be inevitable. When this happens, you must be completely calm and gentle with your partner. If you are angry with them for some reason, you must put this on hold until they've stopped feeling overwhelmed. Otherwise, this will only exacerbate the situation.

How this situation manifests will vary with each person, but the most common response is either crying or going into self-defense mode, as if the trauma is happening again and they must protect themselves. The best thing to do is to offer reassurance and take on a soothing tone of voice. If your partner was a victim of violence, play it safe and do not touch them at all until they are ready. Understand that sometimes our partners may not have obvious signs of being triggered. Instead, they may just become quiet and depressed. It's important to keep an eye out for less noticeable responses if you know they've been exposed to a potential trigger.

What each person needs depends highly on the person and the trauma they experienced. A good rule of thumb is to remove the trigger as soon as possible and do the opposite of what started it.

5. **Know what you can do to help them move on**

If the trauma is severe and very rarely comes up, then it's best to disregard this stage entirely. However, if the trauma is getting in the way of your relationship, or preventing your partner from advancing their life, think of ways to help them make more peace with what happened. This could mean seeking out professional help or coming up with step-by-step solutions amongst yourselves. It's important that these solutions are not just your responsibility; these steps should also challenge your partner to create more healthy response patterns.

Let's go back to the example of the jealous partner. It's not realistic to expect someone to call you every couple of hours every single time they go out drinking. Ideally, the jealous partner should move on from this behavior once the relationship starts to become more long-term. To start this positive transition, they could make calls less frequent during each night out, or they could decide to just text every hour. The jealous partner should come up with steps they can do to avoid feeling low or depressed during these incidents. Perhaps, they could also go out with friends or channel their energy into an intense work-out session. Create a positive new habit to take the place of unhealthy responses. This way, everyone wins.

Chapter Six - It's All About You

We're often told we should find a significant other that loves us as we are. This is true, to an extent. We should all expect our partners to love and accept us for our likes, dislikes, and our positive attributes without trying to change them. They should even love us for our quirks, flaws, and idiosyncrasies. They should love what makes us different. But no partner should ever be expected to put up with negative or destructive behavior that deeply affects them. Your arrogant attitude, your manipulative tendencies, your persistent laziness; none of this is your partner's responsibility and if it hurts them, you'd be cruel to ask them to accept it. Asking our partners to deal with what upsets them and hurts them will inevitably lead to contempt. And contempt is one of the few things a relationship cannot heal from.

The majority of relationships fail because one or both partners refuse to do the self-work. I urge you now to not be the partner that doesn't do the self-work. Don't be the one who doesn't make the effort. You may feel indignant now, but if the relationship ends and you know you didn't try your hardest, you're going to be left drowning in regret. Work on you, before it's too late.

And remember, it doesn't end here. The behavior that hurts your partner now will likely hurt all your future partners to come. As long as you want to be in a happy, healthy relationship, you will continue to need positive self-transformation.

How to Instantly Become a Better Partner

If you want to do right by your partner, implement these easy habits into your dynamic. Create these new communication norms and you'll instantly start to see better results in your relationship.

1. Ask for what you need

Stop expecting your significant other to read your mind. They have their own life, with their own needs, and you can't expect them to sit around trying to guess how you feel. Asking for what you need does not make you needy, it makes you self-aware and emotionally mature. It shows you value your relationship because you're serious about creating better conditions. Instead of expecting your partner to jump through hoops, you are being upfront about how to help. This makes it easy on them. This gives them a real opportunity to adjust their behavior.

When you ask for what you need, you are much more likely to *get* what you need. To get the best outcome from your discussion, remember to use "I feel" statements.

2. Bring up a problem before it gets worse

There are many reasons we avoid bringing up problems. Sometimes it's because we're uncomfortable with confrontation, afraid of the other person's response, or perhaps, we just don't want to admit there's a problem. What usually happens is the problem continues and gets worse. When we avoid bringing up our problems, we risk two things.

- Exploding at our partner when we just can't take it anymore. When we allow ourselves to reach our breaking point, we are more likely to say something harsh that we don't mean. This can upset our significant other and it may even cause lasting damage to the relationship.

- Developing contempt for our partner. If we don't give our partner the opportunity to make it better, it will not get better. This will frustrate us more and more, and eventually lead to resentment. You may find your mind swarming with questions like, "How on earth can he/she not notice? Why isn't he/she more aware of what this is doing to me?" This can spiral into feelings of not feeling cared for, and anger at your partner for putting you through this. Newsflash: you are putting *yourself* through this if you don't tell your partner what's wrong!

3. Pay attention to timing

Always consider the timing of what you do and say to your partner. This makes a massive difference in the response you receive from them. If you're trying to have a serious talk with them, don't do it when they're exhausted from work or if they've had a bad day. This could incite an argument since they're not in their right mind. Always use timing to your advantage. Talk to your partner the morning after they've had a night of great sleep or on a day they seem level-headed.

This rule extends even beyond serious talks and discussions. Whenever you're going to make any decision that impacts both you and your partner, think of where this will fall on their timeline and schedule. If there are days of the year that are particularly hard for your partner (for example, anniversaries of deaths), remember them. Ensure you don't plan any big social events when they would prefer to lay low.

4. Use gentle and constructive language

Mistakes happen. And sometimes our partners don't always have the greatest ideas. Still, you should always make the effort to stay constructive when providing your partner with any feedback. Acknowledge what they did right, but also point out opportunities for growth. If you feel the need to criticize your partner, always reframe your comments from the perspective of how they can improve. If you make them feel like everything they do is wrong, you're not fixing the situation, and you're only disempowering them from cooperating with you. Always focus on solutions.

5. Always listen, always

This one gets repeated a lot, but it's for a good reason. Active listening in our relationship is extremely important. In fact, it is directly linked to the overall quality of communication with our partner. And in an unhappy couple, it is highly common for at least one partner to complain that they don't feel heard and their significant other never listens to them. By listening, we are staying present in the conversation. We are showing our partner respect. And by actively listening, we are also lowering the likelihood of misunderstandings. The next time your partner is speaking, avoid just waiting for your turn to reply and really absorb everything they're saying.

6. Keep your expectations kind and realistic

We all move through life and make progress at different paces. This is no more true for you and your partner. One way you can cause needless disappointment for yourself and hurt for your partner is by expecting far too much from them. If it seems like you're always waiting for your partner to tick off boxes on your checklist, take a step back and re-examine the extent of what you're asking. If you find yourself continuously disappointed, consider why before taking any further action. Are you trying to change their personality? Are you asking for too big of an adjustment too fast? Are your demands being insensitive to their current life circumstances? These are all necessary questions to ask yourself.

Some specific examples of unfair expectations:

- Expecting your partner to be on top of all the chores when someone close to them has just passed away.
- Wanting your partner to become athletic because you are most attracted to athletic people.
- Expecting your partner to cook a wonderful meal and keep the house spotless after a stressful day at work.
- Demanding that your partner immediately become great at that move you like in bed, when they're already giving it their best effort.
- Expecting your partner to have all the same positive qualities as your previous partner.

Please note that these expectations do not apply to matters of compassion, respect, safety, consideration, and kindness. These do not count as high expectations, this is basic human decency. No matter what your partner is going through, they should always be meeting these basic expectations.

7. Stop bringing up the past

To clarify, it's not bringing up the past in itself that's damaging, it's when we dredge up the past to start an argument. If you've already talked about it and your partner has apologized, we shouldn't continue to hold their mistakes against them. If we do this, we're demonstrating we haven't truly forgiven them. As long as we continue to hold this grudge, we are creating negativity in the relationship. Either you should move past this mistake and forgive your partner, or if you can't forgive them, do what needs to be done and end the relationship. Continuing to throw past mistakes in our partner's face is a cruel act as it traps them in the mistake. Not only this, but it increases the likelihood of us getting into circuitous conversations that are never solved. Since we are so attached to the problem, we can never move onto solutions. Stop using the past as a weapon and try your best to move on, if you're deciding to stay.

8. Express gratitude more often

Science has proven that when we approach life with gratitude, we instantly feel happier. Not only does expressing gratitude in our relationships lead to our own happy feelings, but it can be transformative and powerful for our partners. By showing gratitude, we are reminding them of their tremendous worth and highlighting what they are doing right.

Being on the receiving end of gratitude can be incredibly empowering. If your partner is going through a hard time, it will ignite more motivation and progress, ultimately creating more satisfaction in the long run. But most importantly, it shows them that their efforts do not go unseen and that you recognize all they do. This will instantly make them feel more positive and valued. Gratitude is, overall, a big win for everyone. Express it more often! You'll be glad you did. It's as simple as telling your partner "I love you and appreciate you" or highlighting a specific action they did/do and explaining in more detail why you're so grateful for it.

Understanding Your Relationship Attachment Style

Our attachment styles are formed in early childhood and they play a major role in our relationships. According to psychoanalysts, the attachment style we form all comes down to the dynamic we had with our caregivers, during infancy. This style determines our behavior patterns, the types of relationships we're most likely to choose, and essentially how we go about getting our needs met.

No attachment style is 'bad' per se, but some are less conducive to harmonious relationships and more inclined to exhibit unhealthy behavior. In any case, it's always important that we're aware of our attachment style (and our partner's as well) so we can have a better understanding of our behavior patterns and responses.

- **The Anxious-Preoccupied Attachment Style**

Those with this style tend to crave emotional attachment and may have a history of tumultuous relationships. They tend to dislike being alone and are prone to fantasizing about their dream partner. Unfortunately, this attachment style encounters a lot of stressors in a relationship. A lot of these are self-inflicted. During times of emotional distress, they can become jealous, possessive, or needy. They require a lot of love and validation, and they may react negatively if they don't receive reassurance or positive reinforcement.

It can be said that these types live in their heads a lot. They are often their own worst enemy, intensely worried they'll be betrayed. Those with this attachment style make up about 20% of the population.

- **The Dismissive-Avoidant Attachment Style**

Quite the opposite of the Anxious type, the Dismissive-Avoidant is highly self-sufficient. This type displays a great amount of independence and requires a lot of freedom in their relationships. Though they may secretly desire a deep connection, they will appear closed-off and rarely engage deeply in relationships. Many people who date these types end up complaining that they seem emotionally unavailable and at times, even indifferent. It takes more work for them to show vulnerability, and some may even be commitment-phobic. They tend to see intimacy as a loss of their personal freedom.

Avoidant types are so accustomed to taking care of their own needs that they can become plagued by obsessions as a way to self-medicate. This may be substance abuse, or something less damaging like exercise or food. Roughly 23% of the population consists of these types.

- **The Fearful-Avoidant Attachment Style**

This type lives with a lot of conflict. A combination of the previous two styles, the Fearful-Avoidant exhibits a push-pull pattern of behavior. They deeply crave a close connection and yet part of them wants to run away to safety. Unfortunately, this type tends to do both those things. During their worst moments, they may cling to their partner and even appear quite needy. But once their partner gets close to them and comforts them, they may suddenly feel suffocated and trapped. Like Anxious types, the Fearful personalities are also prone to turbulent relationships.

These unpredictable types don't have a fixed strategy for meeting their needs. Their behavior patterns are often a result of trauma from abandonment or abuse. This is the most rare attachment style, making up only 1% of the population.

- **The Secure Attachment Style**

As its name suggests, this attachment style is the most secure of the four, and is widely considered the most emotionally healthy. They have higher levels of emotional intelligence and find it easier to regulate their emotions. Healthy boundaries are easy to set and they have a generally positive outlook on relationships. This type feels secure in a relationship, and they also do just fine on their own. Overall, they tend to be more satisfied in relationships and have a much easier time forming a healthy connection.

The Secure Attachment style is formed when one's childhood is experienced as mostly positive. Caregivers were perceived as secure and safe, so they continue to project this experience onto all future relationships. This is the most common type of all, with 57% of the population characterized as Secure.

Most people don't change their attachment styles, but it is entirely possible to do so. Any individual with one of the less-healthy styles can develop more secure qualities with tremendous self-work. In order for this to happen, however, the individual must pursue therapy and/or seek out the companionship of someone with a secure attachment style. By cultivating self-awareness and a willingness to develop better habits, anyone can transition out of their unhealthy behavior.

Must-Know Tips for Starting a New Relationship When You Have a History of Bad Relationships

Do you have one of the first three attachment styles? If so, you've probably had a few bad relationships, maybe even abusive relationships. You may be working through some negative or even outright destructive behavior, but rest assured, it is possible to move on. Plenty of people have done it on their own. And with a loving companion by your side, you can work on it together.

The trauma we endure can shape the way we communicate with our partners and the imagined stressors we're more likely to experience. For this reason, we may express more fear, anger, or distress in situations that would not normally upset someone. This isn't always fair on our partners, especially since they aren't the ones that hurt us, and it's important we don't become abusive ourselves or cause our new partners pain. Keep the following tips in mind to maintain your emotional and mental health, while also being considerate of your partner.

Please note that if your trauma is severe, these tips are not meant to substitute for help from a mental health professional.

1. **Make a list of behavior you will no longer tolerate**

In order to turn over a new leaf successfully, it's essential that we identify what we wish to remove from our lives. If you've had a history of experiencing pain, make a list of behavior in previous partners that caused you significant pain. This list is exactly what you should no longer tolerate in relationships from now on. There's no way to make excuses for future abusive partners because this list makes it simple; they either did it or they didn't. Refer back to it to remind yourself of its contents and feel free to show it to new partners once you're seriously dating.

Having this list is also helpful because during times of emotional distress, our feelings can cloud our judgment. It can save us from directing unwarranted anger or upset at partners who didn't do anything wrong. For example, if you're having a bad day, you may feel more suspicious or anxious than usual. If your partner does something, you may overreact. Looking back at your list, you'll see that your partner didn't actually exhibit the behavior you outlined. This will make it clear that the feeling likely comes from within, because you're having a bad day.

For this list to be truly successful, we should strictly write down behavior and not emotions. Adding to your list that you will not tolerate anyone causing you pain makes things tricky;

sometimes we can impose pain on ourselves and mistakenly believe it is the fault of our partners. And feel free to get an outside opinion on whether the behavior noted down is sufficient and reasonable.

2. When you're ready, share what happened with your new partner

In order for our partners to support us in the best way possible, they need to know what they're dealing with. Without knowledge of what happened and how it affected us, they'll have no clue how to help. Share with them what happened, what you need from them, and what you're doing to help yourself move on.

If you're not ready to tell them just yet, then wait till you're ready, but in the meantime, don't expect them to just *know* how to help. If you don't think you'll be ready to share with them any time soon, feel free to ask a friend to tell your new partner. Although this isn't the ideal way of letting them know, it is better than leaving them in the dark. All in all, it's always best for your new partner to have as much information as possible so they can offer the exact support you need.

3. Rely on your support system whenever necessary

Our closest friends and family are our greatest allies. If you're ever unsure, use them as your sounding board and ask them for an outside opinion. Our feelings are not always trustworthy since past trauma makes us more predisposed to feel a certain way. Ask someone you trust who can give you a neutral opinion. Don't make all the big decisions on your own.

Furthermore, it's also essential that the person you're relying on for advice is someone whose love life you seek to emulate. Opinions are not all made equal. If a person in a healthy relationship gives you one piece of advice, but ten people in bad relationships say the opposite, you should always listen to the person who has lived the outcome you most desire. Look for the most neutral people possible; if you struggle with jealousy, don't get advice from someone who also struggles with jealousy.

4. Resist making comparisons to previous partners

When we're in a new relationship, it is completely natural for our brains to use past relationships and partners as reference points. This is just what the brain does to try and understand a new situation. Although the instinct is natural, keep in mind that its analyses are not always correct. When we encounter new territory, our past experiences are a highly limited pool of knowledge to extrapolate from.

Make the effort to remind yourself that your current partner is not your previous partner. Your brain will try to make comparisons, but resist them when you can. If the attitude your new partner exhibits is different to what you previously experienced, then remind yourself there's no reason to expect the same outcome. If there's no real evidence, there's no reason to believe the worst. If your previous partner cheated on you with a friend of the opposite sex, remember that there are many individuals who don't do this. There's no reason to become angry or upset right off-the-bat. Your current partner did not hurt you like your previous partner, so do not punish them for something they didn't do.

It is especially important that we don't vocalize any comparisons to previous partners. If our current partner did nothing wrong, this will come across as very insulting. If you get the urge to do this in the heat of the moment, resist it at all costs.

5. Do not expect your partner to fix everything for you

You should definitely expect support from your partner during times of healing. However, there's a big difference between support and an emotional or psychological crutch. Support crosses the line into 'crutch' territory when you stop doing things for yourself. Instead of doing the self-work to transform your behavior and thinking patterns, you expect your partner to change *their* behavior. There is suddenly intense pressure on the 'crutch' partner to fix everything and if anything goes wrong, it automatically becomes their fault. Avoid this dynamic at all costs! This is a sure way to get your partner to resent you and no one would blame them – forcing someone to be your crutch is cruel!

When we engage in dynamics like this, we immediately become stagnant. Since someone else is babying us, we are never challenged, and this means we won't grow. Remember that feeling uncomfortable isn't always bad. We should always examine our discomforts and see if it's something we can work on, before asking someone to change. Don't expect your partner to meet all your needs (and more!) without meeting any of theirs in return. A history of bad relationships is not a good excuse to take advantage of a new partner.

6. Start making self-care an essential part of your routine

One powerful thing we can do for ourselves is engage in self-care practices. Ditch the idea that self-care is only for special occasions and incorporate it into your daily or weekly routine. Self-care does not have to cost any money; it just means you're allowing yourself to do whatever it is that makes you feel calm and taken care of. You know it's self-care when you reconnect to who you are and when you feel at peace. This can mean taking a warm bubble bath and listening to your favorite music. Or this can mean going to a relaxing cafe, journaling, and reading a great book or treating yourself to some baked goods.

If you've got a bigger budget, you can get a massage and indulge in chocolate. The possibilities are endless!

When we start making self-care part of our routine, we also rewire our brain to feel its effects more often. It's not just the bubble bath or massage that becomes the new norm, the peace and calm becomes more of a norm as well. This is essential when we're recovering from trauma because we are in deep need of rewiring responses and impulses. In addition to this, however, it is a powerful symbol for the new chapter you will begin. By carving out time to focus on you, you are vowing to start thinking of your needs more often. You are recognizing your importance and you are saying no to relationships that cause you pain. Self-care for the win.

Chapter Seven - The Ticking Time Bomb

When we're considering potential partners, we tend to put too much weight in excitement and passion. While that's, no doubt, extremely important, we neglect what really makes the meat of a relationship. Almost anyone can bring a fun time to the table, but what will they do during the hard times? The dark nights when an argument goes round in circles? When voices are raised and it feels like your blood is boiling? The way you and your partner behave and react in these situations has the biggest bearing on your relationship. Your sex life and the number of interests you have in common: neither of these factors are a true test of your strength as a team. The biggest signifier of your relationship's strength is how you fight and how you find solutions to problems.

Even if you're soulmates and you have a blast together every single day, there are going to be days and nights where you can't stand each other. While no one is perfect at the beginning of a relationship, it is essential that we learn over time. There will come a time when we need to handle a ticking time bomb (a highly sensitive situation) and in order to prevent it from exploding, the necessary knowledge and tools are required. Expect that challenges will arise and be prepared to solve them.

When to Press the Pause or Stop Button

Open communication can solve many problems, but there are times when you need to take a step back. Talking doesn't always make things better, sometimes it can cause damage and needless distress. If it's an important discussion, then press the pause button and resume the talk when both parties are more level-headed. If the conversation isn't about anything important, press stop and drop the topic like a hot potato. These are the signs you need to cool off and let it sit:

- **Emotions are running high**

If there are tears, raised voices, and you get the distinct feeling someone (and this includes you) might explode, press that pause button. When emotions get too charged and intense, there's a higher likelihood of someone boiling over and saying something hurtful. You may even make a decision you can't take back. To press pause successfully, say something like:

"I sense we're both getting too consumed by our emotions. Why don't we settle down and resume this conversation later? I want to solve this problem and in our current state, I don't think we can."

Once both parties have had a chance to cool off, you'll come back more rational and level-headed. A potential disaster will have been averted and you'll feel grateful for taking that break.

- **You've had this conversation before and it didn't end well**

For many couples, there can be recurring discussions that never seem to get solved. Some of these can bring out the worst in both partners and end in bitter, hurtful remarks that do a lot of damage. If you find this dead-end discussion cropping up again, nip it in the bud while you can. Consider saying:

"The last time we had this talk, we both said a lot of things we didn't mean. I feel that it did more harm than good, and I really don't want to see that situation repeated. I really want to fix this situation so how about we take some time to think about solutions? We can each think of ways to move forward. And we can resume this discussion when we have new ideas to bring to the table."

If the discussion has no bearing on the relationship, simply point out what happened last time, and say you feel it's best to agree to disagree. Each couple will have their own versions of dead-end topics, and you need to learn when it's not important to win.

- **At least one partner is tired**

When we're tired, we can sometimes lose the energy required to regulate ourselves and our emotions. That's not to say the emotions we feel when we are tired aren't real. In fact, oftentimes this can display what we really feel – but we become less able to deal with them maturely and effectively. When we have energy, our brain can easily go through the process of organizing our words and thoughts in a clear, constructive manner. When we don't have energy, our brains can fail to get this process started or do it properly.

When we enter an argument in this tired state, we are not using the best tools we have. We are not equipped to be in the arena and it's best we get out before we cause damage. In this state of mind, we are much more likely to overreact and say something we don't mean. We shouldn't always expect our partners to understand that we're just tired and move on. If what we say is genuinely hurtful, it can cause deep hurt. Do not get into serious talks with your partner when one partner cannot communicate effectively in that moment.

- **Words have started to get hurtful**

For one reason or another, a conversation can really start to sour. You'll know this is starting to happen because either your partner will say something that stings or you'll say something you normally wouldn't say. If you notice that tone and language are starting to get aggressive or mean, then you need to walk away immediately and cool off. This is the point in our arguments that we should always try to avoid. Our heated conversations should never hurt. And if it does, know that it has gone too far.

Don't just walk out without saying a word, as this will appear as storming off, which could only further anger your partner. Instead, point out to your partner that you've started to say things you don't mean, and emphasize that you don't want to co-create a situation that does lasting damage. Suggest that you both take time to calm down and think about more constructive ways of getting your points across.

- **The conversation is going around in circles**

This often happens when both partners are tired, especially when they've exhausted themselves by having such a drawn-out argument. You'll notice that the same points continue to be raised, the same responses made each time, and yet somehow you keep coming back to the same thing over and over.

This is a sign your conversation has gone around in circles. If someone doesn't end it soon, it will only continue to go on and on, and a solution will likely never be found. Try to point out the conversation has become circuitous as soon as you notice. It could end with hurtful statements made, but even if it doesn't, it's a huge waste of time and energy for both partners.

If you find a certain topic leads you around in circles a lot, consider having this conversation via email. When discussions are written out, it's much easier to see where the confusion lies. By examining the responses closely, it becomes clear why the discussion always becomes circuitous.

- **The outcome of the discussion won't actually affect the relationship**

If the conversation is getting heated, consider whether the topic actually matters. Let's say you've both started to argue about a topic on the news. Ask yourself what difference it makes if you both agree or disagree. Does disagreeing on this topic make you have less fun together? Does it hurt you in any way? Does it affect either of your abilities to be good partners for one another? If the answer is 'no' to all of these questions, then this topic is not that important. The outcome does not affect your relationship in any way – so don't rile yourselves up over nothing.

How to Bring Up Your Concerns the Right Way

If you're going to be in a happy, healthy relationship, you need to know how to raise your concerns the right way. In other words, without causing significant damage to your partner and while being honest enough to incite change. These are incredibly sensitive situations, so pay close attention to the following tips:

- **Choose timing carefully**

Remember what we said about paying attention to timing? That's even more important when we're about to have a big talk. Don't bring up serious conversations when your partner is having a bad day or when they are exhausted. This will not lead to a favorable outcome! You're best bet is always to approach your partner when they are rested, calm, and not going through a difficult time.

- **Resist saying "but..." to soften the blow**

We always think we're doing someone a favor by starting with a positive before getting to the negative – but this is actually not true. Take, for example, the statement: "I love how passionate you've become about home-decorating and I think you've got some great ideas, but I'm just not sure I like these new changes."

As soon as the "but" comes into play, the earlier part of the sentence doesn't mean anything. It can be even more upsetting because you've gotten your partner's hopes up by starting with something so positive, but these hopes are completely trampled on by the time you finish the sentence. Your partner is smart! They know the real point is everything that comes after the "but." Don't try to soften the blow with this (bad) technique, and instead do it through careful language. Speaking of which...

- **Utilize all you've learned about gentle and constructive language**

We brought up constructive language in an earlier chapter, and it's time to put that lesson to good use. This is the perfect time to use your "I" or "I feel" statements! Instead of voicing your concerns in terms of what your partner did, reframe them so it's about what you feel. Steer clear of absolute language and assumptions, and ensure no sentence starts with "you."

If you're upset about how they rarely help with chores, resist the urge to say, "You never help with chores and you don't care about how it affects me." Instead, try saying something like, "I feel like I'm not getting enough help with chores. I'd feel a lot better if we could have a more even distribution of tasks." Notice that there is no mention of "you" at all. This is ideal because your partner doesn't feel cornered and it doesn't make any assumptions. We are also reducing the chance of an argument because it's difficult to argue with how someone feels. That's their reality.

- **Prepare for pushback or questions**

You should always prepare for the possibility of your partner pushing back a little. This doesn't necessarily mean it'll be with anger or frustration, but if you think there's a chance it might happen, then definitely prepare for it. Consider all the ways your partner might try to argue with it and think of a constructive, confident answer. This is especially important if you're the more submissive partner and you have a tendency to give in. For example, the second partner in the previous scenario might say, "But I washed the dishes last week" or "But I'm not as good at doing chores as you." You know your partner well enough to anticipate with some accuracy what their protests might be. Even if their responses are infuriating, stay calm and constructive.

- **Conclude with solutions and positivity**

Don't just sit and stew in the problem at hand, be ready to come up with a solution. Your partner may have some ideas as well, but for the best outcome, bring your own ideas to the table. Think of the next step and give your partner a place to start. This is the best way to work through a concern because you're essentially saying "This problem is easy to solve and here, this is the perfect opportunity. We can start making things better right now!"

Going back to our example problem, the concerned partner could then say, "I think a great way to resolve this would be to take turns each week doing the chores. How about I do the rest of this week and you can start on Monday?" Notice how this makes the situation instantly seem more positive. The problem is not the point anymore, it's the solution.

As we mentioned in a previous point, it's not a good idea to start the discussion with a "but" statement where you go from positive to negative – but the reverse is a much better idea. Add the positive statement to the end of the conversation so it can end on a good note.

5 Statements to Instantly Defuse a Heated Discussion

It happens in every relationship. Sometimes you find yourself in a talk with your partner that's gone from perfectly chill to blazing hot – and not in a good way. Perhaps it's because they've just had a hard day and they're in a bad mood, or perhaps they just woke up on the wrong side of the bed. Whatever it is, you can't seem to tame the fire in their attitude and all you know is it needs to stop now. Keep these statements in your back pocket to immediately calm a heated situation:

1. "I see your point."

When we say this, we validate our partner's point of view. This can calm someone down because all we really want is to make our point understood. We continue arguing because we want to make ourselves heard. Eliminate the need to continue arguing, by saying they have already made themselves heard.

2. "I understand."

This statement is ideal for defusing a situation without giving in. By saying you understand you are not admitting you are wrong; you are just saying you comprehend their view. Similar to the previous statement, you are letting them know what they've said has been thoughtfully received.

3. "What can I do to make it better?"

Instead of fueling the argument, try shifting the conversation to possible solutions. Without stirring the pot, you're letting your partner know you're ready to fix the situation. This will make them more willing to cooperate. This statement works wonders, but you must be willing to put in extra work. Since you are letting your partner know you want to make things better, you need to follow up on that promise.

4. "What do you need right now?"

Like the previous response, you're skipping the argument and going straight to the solution. Your partner will be more touched by this question because you're asking them directly what they need. This can cut to the core of an argument because you're saying, "I know it's not really about this. I know it's about you, and what you're not getting. I want to take care of that." Take on a more nurturing attitude and be willing to do what your partner says they need.

5. **"I'm sorry."**

Don't underestimate the power of apologies. It can whittle a fiery blaze down to a single burning ember. Sometimes, it's just not worth arguing till our heads turn blue. Apologizing is not always about admitting defeat or letting your partner win, it's about choosing harmony over your ego. It doesn't always mean "You're right, I'm wrong" sometimes it can mean "It hurts me to see you so upset and I'm sorry you feel this way."

What NOT to Say During an Argument

We've covered what you should say. Now, let's get to what you definitely shouldn't say. If you're in a heated discussion or an argument, steer clear of the following phrases and sentences if you want to prevent an explosion.

1. **"Calm down."**

It's a big claim, but I'll say it: never in the history of mankind has an urge to "calm down" actually calmed an upset person down. Even if you mean well, this comes off as condescending and unsympathetic. The person who needs to calm down is actually in deep need of empathy and understanding; this statement demonstrates the opposite of that. It shows that the non-upset person doesn't understand at all, since they think it should be so easy for their partner to stop expressing their emotions in that moment. If you say this, you will not get a positive response. Avoid it at all costs and instead try asking them to share more with you.

2. "Not this again!"

If your partner is upset and you bemoan the fact they're upset about something *again,* this will only create more anger. By saying this, we're invalidating our partner. We're showing annoyance and impatience at their true feelings. We're essentially saying we don't care because they've been upset about it before. Instead of showing care, we are being condescending and implying their reaction is ridiculous.

3. "If you don't _____ then I'm breaking up with you."

This is a big no-no in relationships. In fact, many people consider it emotional abuse. If you're threatening your partner with a break-up in order to get them to do something, you're displaying cruel behavior, especially if you're not really serious. Even if you are, however, phrasing it as a threat could still cause a lot of damage. If your partner stops whatever they're doing and you continue to be in a relationship, this moment will leave them with a lot of anxiety. They will begin to feel as if they're walking on eggshells. If they start to make changes for you, they will only be acting out of fear, instead of love.

To properly convey how you feel without resorting to threats, remember to use "I" statements. Instead of saying, "If you don't stop talking to him, I'm breaking up with you" try saying, "I feel very upset by how much you talk to this other guy. It's starting to bother me on a deep level and I worry it's affecting my ability to be a healthy partner for you."

9 Relationship Problems You Cannot Fix

Try as hard as you may, there are some issues in a relationship that cannot be helped nine out of ten times. You may be a master communicator, and perhaps even your partner as well, but sometimes, there's only so much you can do. If your relationship has any of the following problems, it may be best to walk away before both partners begin to hurt.

1. **Serial cheating**

One instance of infidelity can really tear a relationship to shreds, but even then, it's salvageable – if the cheating partner makes lasting changes to their behavior. But continuous infidelity is a different issue. This indicates the cheating partner has a real problem, and they can't be in a healthy relationship until they solve it on their own. Stop making allowances for a partner that constantly cheats on you. It will only lead to more pain. No amount of good communication will fix this. It is entirely up to the cheating partner to do the self-work. And if they haven't started now, why wait around and continue to get hurt?

2. Too much contempt

It's normal to be mad at your partner for something, but contempt is a different story. Contempt runs deeper and is far more persistent. It happens when one partner can't let something go. It's begun to gnaw at them, they can't forget it or forgive, and it's caused resentment to build. The fault could be anyone's. It could be the non-contemptuous partner's fault for deeply hurting his or her partner, or it could be the contemptuous partner's fault for refusing to heal and let go. A little scorn is normal after an upsetting event, but it transforms into contempt when time has passed, and time has healed no wounds whatsoever.

3. Narcissistic personality disorder

There's a big difference between being a narcissist and being a clinical Narcissist, i.e. having Narcissistic Personality Disorder. If your partner is a little vain, occasionally makes big-headed statements, but can still take accountability for his mistakes, then your partner is likely just a regular lowercase narcissist. They may be annoying sometimes, but they don't have a personality disorder, and you can still make progress with them. A Narcissist, on the other hand, cannot be fixed and it's best to step away now before you get more hurt. Clinical Narcissists are unable to take accountability for anything and they have an unwillingness to recognize the needs of other people. It is not possible for them to be in a healthy, happy relationship.

4. Conflicting goals

You may have all the same common interests, but at the end of the day, conflicting goals can be a killer. Some partners may be lucky enough to settle on a compromise, but some goals are on opposite ends of the spectrum. If you desperately want kids and your partner doesn't want them at all, there's no way to compromise on this. Unless someone changes their mind, both partners cannot get what they want and this means one partner is doomed to feel unsatisfied. This can lead to resentment and may even ruin a connection. In the end, it can result not only in pain, but a lot of wasted time.

5. Abuse

If one partner engages in abusive behavior, whether physical or emotional, the relationship should end as soon as possible. Abusive behavior is toxic and will only drag both partners into a cycle of pain that continues on until it's off-the-charts. The abusive partner is always at fault and their behavior demonstrates they are incapable of being in a healthy relationship at the current stage in their life. It is advised that this partner leaves the relationship, stops hurting the other partner, and pursues therapy so they evolve into more healthy, loving companion.

The abusive partner is less likely to admit what they're doing is a problem, so it may be up to the abused partner to find the strength to leave. Friends and family are in the best position to end such a volatile relationship. If you are close to someone who is suffering from abuse, see if you can assist in getting them out of the bad situation.

6. Failure to grow

Conflict is a natural part of any relationship, and if both partners are healthy, they should be finding ways to achieve better harmony. For one reason or another, however, one or both partners may find there's a persistent lack of growth. In other words, there's a quality or behavior pattern that has continued to have a negative effect without any improvement, even though our partner knows we want to see change. This is only a big problem if the behavior that needs to be grown out of is affecting the happiness of the relationship.

For example, if your partner has been working on his anger issues for years but is still as turbulent as he was in the beginning, reconsider whether you can put up with this for the future to come. If your partner continues to flirt with other people even though you've repeatedly pointed out it bothers you, it's likely this will not ever change. At a certain point, it becomes clear when certain issues are here to stay and it's important that we make the right decision concerning our future. Either this behavior is too deeply ingrained in their personalities or they aren't motivated to seek out this growth. Choose what's right for your sanity and stop waiting for change that likely won't come.

7. Constant and pointless arguing

We may go through periods of bickering with our partners – especially if we're going through a rough patch in our lives – but if this occurrence is persistent and a constant drain on your energy, it's time to stop and think. Frequent pointless arguing is often a sign of a much deeper problem. Sometimes both partners have stopped being compatible, fallen out of love, or have developed deep resentment for each other. It's very rare that these problems can be fixed. If it has become easier to be apart from your partner than be with them, it may be time to put a cork in it.

8. Inability to trust

It's true what they say; without trust, a relationship is nothing. Trust forms the foundation of every relationship. And without a strong foundation, it doesn't matter how glamorous and impressive the rest of it is, it'll come crumbling down as soon as the wind changes. Once trust is broken, it's extremely difficult to rebuild. It can take years and a lot of hard work if a couple decides to try and make it work, and even then, sometimes it is not successful. In every relationship, we should have the basic assurance that our partner won't hurt or betray us. Consider how deeply broken the trust is and whether you ever see yourself fully recovering.

9. Deep feelings for a third party

We can all get over lust or a mild crush, but if it's more than that, we're dealing with something else entirely. Sometimes, the feelings one partner has for a third party are very deep, and they may even be verging on love. For feelings to get to this point, the partner in question would have to be exposed to this third party for an extended period of time. We know this because it takes a while for deep feelings to develop.

There's a lot less hope for the relationship if the partner in question has been intentionally seeking out the company of this third party. This behavior displays a big problem with self-control – and this could pose a serious problem to the relationship down the road. If this scenario takes place, it may be beneficial for the relationship to end.

It's a slightly different story if the partner with feelings has developed them due to involuntary exposure, for example, through work. In this case, it is not a self-control issue and there is hope. The only way to fix it, however, is by completely removing oneself from all situations involving the third party. If this is a co-worker, it means making a big decision, such as quitting the job causing exposure. Otherwise, these feelings will only grow.

The good news is that the majority of partners can, indeed, work through their problems. If your relationship issue wasn't listed, there are higher chances for you working out your issues. And while the problems listed are mostly unfixable, there will always be exceptions. In any case, it always takes a lot of hard work, kind communication, and incredible cooperation to see positive change.

Chapter Eight - Deepening the Bond

There's always more we can do to deepen the bond in our relationship. At the end of the day, we shouldn't just feel like lovers; we should also feel like friends and to an extent, family. When we feel a strong connection to our partners, there is a much higher likelihood that communication will be kind, helpful, and transformative. And in addition to this, a good connection means we're much more likely to follow up on our compromises and be a better partner. When we feel close to someone, we instantly feel more compassionate and empathetic. These two qualities are necessary for a loving connection.

As excellent as these bonding techniques may be, they require commitment from both partners to be completely effective. A positive outcome takes effort and attention; it does not simply fall into your lap after one attempt. Keep these activities and exercises in mind for the rest of your future to come. Even when relationship communication is good, this is no reason to stop seeking out opportunities to bond.

Exercises and Activities that Strengthen Relationships

- **Start a love journal with your partner**

This practice does wonders for maintaining romantic connections. Start off by purchasing a journal (ideally together) that you both love the look of. If you don't live together, then aim to take turns with the journal. Come up with a schedule that works for you. Will the journal pass hands weekly? Fortnightly? Whenever you feel like it? Whatever works for you!

If you do live together, keep the journal in a private area of the house, but one where you frequently pass by. Again, the arrangement of who and when to write is up to you. I advise writing something every day, even if it's very short, or taking turns. If you decide to take turns, find a creative way to indicate who the last writer was, without opening the book. This will ensure you aren't constantly checking it to see if it's been updated.

What's great about this activity is that you can make the rules. Will the book be filled with love letters? Will it all be written in haikus? If one partner is upset, should they write an honest, open letter about how they feel in the journal? Or will this only be reserved for romance? It's totally up to you.

- **Role reversal**

This exercise is great for when two people are trying to see eye-to-eye on a problem. For this exercise to succeed, you and your partner should both be calm and willing to fully cooperate. If there's a hint of snark or sarcasm, abandon the attempt and try again during a better mood.

In this role reversal exercise, you and your partner will have a conversation about a problem at hand, but you'll both speak from the other person's point-of-view. Each of you should really think about what the other partner would say and consider real reasons they might use. One of the reasons this exercise is so effective is because it eliminates the need to "win" the discussion. Partners are forced to think deeply about their loved one's perspective, and this instantly helps couples empathize with each other.

- **The eye contact exercise**

For this exercise, you and your partner should sit across from each other. Ideally, lights should be dim and you should be close to each other, but not too close. Wherever you choose to sit, make sure it's comfortable. It's also important there's no talking or touching during this exercise.

Set a timer for five minutes and aim to look into each others' eyes for the full length of those five minutes. Eye contact should be gentle and uninterrupted. Do not stare intensely at your partner and always remember to blink as you would normally.

You might be surprised by how fast five minutes goes by. Couples can get so lost that they actually lose track of time. After this exercise, you'll feel a heightened sense of connection and attunement with your partner. If a distance has grown between the two of you, this exercise can help bring you back to the same wavelength.

- **Create a vision board**

Get creative with your partner and work on a vision board together. A vision board is a motivational collage of photos, notes, and anything that gets across the future you'd most like to have together. This can include places you'd like to travel to or photos of your dream house together. Whatever fills you both with hope, joy, and positivity about what's to come. It's important that both partners contribute something to this vision board. Remember that it's your *shared* vision, not just one partner's fantasy. And most of all, have fun with it. This is an incredibly fun way to strengthen your connection with your partner. You don't need an artistic streak to enjoy it!

- **Go through the famous '36 Questions that Lead to Love'**

In a famous experiment conducted by psychologists, a significant number of people felt a stronger connection after going through a series of questions together. Many of them even claimed to have fallen in love. Ultimately, the experiment proves that when both partners are engaging in personal self-disclosure, acting vulnerably, and actively listening to their partner, an immediate connection is formed. By forcing two people to do just this, a sense of closeness and intimacy was fostered. Although this experiment was conducted on people who didn't know each other, existing couples still benefit greatly from this bonding exercise.

The 36 questions are separated into three sets, which each one becoming more personal than the last. Take turns answering these questions:

Set 1

1. Whom would you invite to be your dinner guest, given the choice of absolutely anyone in the world?
2. Would you like to be famous? If so, in what way?
3. Before making a phone call, do you rehearse what you're going to say? If so, why do you do this?
4. What constitutes a perfect day in your eyes?
5. When was the last time you sang to yourself? And when was the last time you sang for someone else?

6. If you lived to the age of 90 and had the choice of either the body or mind of a 30-year old for the last 60-years of your life, which would you choose?

7. Do you have any idea how you might die?

8. List three things that you and your partner seem to have in common.

9. What are you most grateful for about your life?

10. If you could change anything at all about the way you were raised, what would you change?

11. Share your life story in as much detail as possible but take only 4 minutes and no longer.

12. If you could acquire any quality or ability overnight, what would you choose?

Set 2

13. If you came upon a crystal ball that could tell you any truth about your life, yourself, your future, or anything else, what would you most want to know?

14. Is there anything that you've dreamed of doing for a long time but haven't ever done? Why haven't you done it yet?

15. What would you say is the greatest accomplishment of your life?

16. What are the qualities and behaviors you most value in a friendship?

17. Talk about your most treasured memory.

18. Now talk about your worst memory.

19. If you knew that you'd die suddenly in a year, is there anything you'd change about the way you're living now? What would that be and why?

20. Describe what friendship means to you.

21. How important are love and affection to you? What roles do they play in your life?

22. Take turns sharing a positive characteristic about each other. Each partner should share five things for a total of ten.

23. How close is your family? Are you warm towards each other? Do you think your childhood was happier than the average childhood?

24. What's your relationship with your mother like? How do you feel about it?

Set 3

25. Take turns sharing three statements, each one beginning with "we." For example, "we're in this room feeling..."

26. Finish this sentence: "I wish I had someone with whom I could share..."

27. If you and your partner were to become close friends, what would be important for them to know?

28. Tell your partner what you honestly like them. This time, try and share something you wouldn't normally say to someone you'd just met.

29. Talk about one of the most embarrassing moments of your life.

30. When was the last time you cried in front of another person? When was the last time you cried by yourself?

31. Share something that you like about your partner already.

32. In your opinion, what is too serious to be joked about, if anything?

33. If you were to die tonight without the opportunity to communicate with anyone, what would you most regret

not having told someone? Why haven't you told them yet?

34. Your house, containing everything you own, catches fire. You've saved your loved ones and pets, and now you only have time to save one more item. What would you save? Why?

35. Of all the people in your family, whose death upset and disturb you the most? Why?

36. Share a personal problem with your partner and ask for their advice on how they might handle it. After this, the partner who offered advice should reflect how the asker seems to be feeling about the chosen problem.

Bond Instantly with these 8 Fun Couple Activities

When it comes down to it, the secret to nurturing your bond is stepping outside of your comfort zone and giving your partner your full attention. Feel free to seek that out in any way you choose, but I highly advise starting with these highly effective methods well known for strengthening bonds instantly.

1. **Massaging each other**

This highly sensual act does more than heat things up, it also asks each partner to engage in a few moments of total kindness towards their loved one. For the length of each massage, one partner is giving completely to their partner without getting anything in return. They are focused on their partner's pleasure entirely and concerned only with creating an enjoyable experience for them through the power of touch. People are so accustomed to physical intimacy and touch strictly being part of sex that it can be wildly exciting to have both those things without sexual contact. This closeness through non-sexual touch is what creates the bond. For the best outcome, both partners should take turns and each massage should take the same length of time.

2. Go out dancing

Dancing is about as close as you can get to sexual intercourse without actually having it! For that reason, dancing can be a real fire-starter in a relationship; not just in the passion department, but even in terms of our connection. It doesn't matter what language you speak or what culture you're from, dancing has a knack for inducing joy and releasing tension in the body. When we do this with our partner, we're expressing ourselves without saying a word. The act of moving in alignment and in rhythm with each other is its own collaborative exercise, and it can be a wonderful symbol for loving each other in harmony. If you and your partner are on the shier side, why not have a drink or two to open you up?

3. Work out together

Believe it or not, numerous studies have proven that working out with your partner boosts overall happiness in your relationship. Researchers have found that this is particularly true for exercises that require both partners to get up and move together in some fashion. Bonding happens at a subconscious level when we engage in the mirror effect. This is the neurological process that leads to bonding and manifests as mirrored movements. By coordinating our actions or mirroring each other's movements, we are firing off mirror neurons and subsequently, deepening our bond.

And that's not all! Studies have also found that working out with a partner leads to improved workout performances. When someone is watching, we are more likely to push harder to try and avoid looking weak. Bond harder and get hotter: doesn't that sound like a great idea?

4. Go on a fancy date

The reason fancy dates have such a positive effect is simple: it gets us out of our routine and forces us to make ourselves look good for our partner. It's no secret that when we take care of ourselves and our appearance, our partner will find us more attractive. Couple this with an exciting scenario you don't normally experience and *voila,* you've started to reboot your connection. If your relationship has started to feel too comfortable, then consider taking your partner out to a nice restaurant. The formality of a fancy date offers a refreshing change from lounging around in sweatpants and it can instantly spice up a boring relationship.

5. Visit the location of one of your "firsts"

Every couple has a unique love story. Even if it wasn't love at first sight or you had an unconventional start, it can be nice to take a walk down memory lane every once in a while. Why not visit the place where you met or where you had your first kiss? Retracing our steps can remind us of how far we've come with our significant other. If you do this with your partner, you'll relive the rush and the butterflies for just a moment; places attached to strong memories inevitably send us back in time. Enjoy these memories with each other and savor the beauty of your one-of-a-kind story, even if it wasn't perfect. Remember that at one point in time, where you are now was where you hoped to be.

6. Go on a trip together

A study conducted by the U.S. Travel Association found that couples who travel together are a great deal more satisfied in their relationships than those who don't. Still, many couples are hesitant to go on a trip because they're convinced that doing this will drain their bank account. This isn't true at all.

To experience the benefits of travel, all couples need to do is to get out of their comfort zone (not just psychologically but geographically as well!) and see something new and exciting. If you've got the budget for it, then sure, visit Paris or Rome, but you can have just as much fun going on a road trip to the next state over. Visit a National Park and stay at a 2 or 3-star hotel, or a humble inn. Get out into nature. Do something you don't normally do. This change of scenery can provide a much needed break from your rigid routine and you'll find your bond deepening naturally as you experience the wider world together.

7. Visit an amusement park

Kid or not, let's face it, amusement parks are incredibly fun. If you don't have a crippling fear of heights, take a break from your routine and spend a day at one with your significant other. Your relationship will see a number of benefits. For starters, thrilling rides will give you a rush of endorphins, meaning you'll feel overcome with happy feelings and a natural high. You'll also be pumped through with adrenaline, a neurotransmitter which is known to create memories in the mind. This means the wonderful day you've had will be solidified in your mind as a happy memory. Since you and your partner are encountering anxiety-inducing situations, you'll bond as you both seek out comfort and warmth in each other.

8. Cook together

If you're on a budget, cooking together is a great way to deepen the bond while also filling the belly. Cooking requires both partners to cooperate and work towards a common goal – exactly what being in a successful relationship is all about! This is great practice for getting in the right mindset for problem-solving and teamwork. Each partner is making their own contribution and the process challenges both partners to get on the same page, or the entire meal suffers.

A cooking project teaches us skills we need to bring into the rest of our relationship. And on top of this, we bond because we're creating something together. We're combining efforts for a tangible finished product. If we succeed in making a delicious meal, couples can bond over the shared pride. They'll likely feel like they can do anything as a team. But those who don't succeed, should not feel discouraged. This is not a reflection on your relationship; you may just need some more cooking practice!

Scroll through cooking websites or recipe books and decide on a meal that you'd like to recreate. This should be something you both love. If you're not experienced cooks, choose a dish with simple-enough instructions that you understand and make sure you possess all the necessary equipment.

Even the closest couples need to take time out to deepen their bond. It doesn't mean it's not already deep, it's about reaching out and reconnecting to remind yourselves why you're there. Time and routine can wear us down; seek out moments of intimacy to strengthen your bond. When we act from a place of deep bonding, relationship communication is more likely to be loving and effective.

Keep an open heart and be brave enough to leave your comfort zone so as to meet each other's need for adventure and variety. Instead of feeling mindless panic in an uncertain scenario, try and transform that feeling into the desire to problem-solve with your partner. Approach life with the mindset that you can do anything if you put your heads together, and you can solve any need you have, if you put your hearts together.

Conclusion

Congratulations on making it to the end of *Relationship Communication*! Whether you realize it or not, you've made one giant leap in the right direction. This isn't just fantastic for you, but for your significant other. You'll both see benefits that impact your day-to-day habits and with continued practice of these techniques, the days of strained communication will feel long gone. By completing this book, you've demonstrated your commitment to more effective and loving communication – and this is one of the best things you could possibly do for the person you love. You're on the right track towards a stronger relationship. You should be proud of yourself!

While you've made a big first step, it's essential that you don't quit now. Relationship communication is an ongoing journey; you've been granted the tools and techniques, but now it's time to use them in real situations, in the real world. Don't make this a short-lived attempt, but incorporate these transformative practices into your daily life and make them last. Reinvent your norms entirely and create exemplary habits.

Make sure you understand the five vital needs that your relationship must fulfill for both partners to be happy. Perhaps work with your partner on identifying which of your needs have been fully met and which ones still remain unmet. This is an essential step to make before finding a solution. Once you've done this, assess your situation and see if you can figure out which stage your relationship is in. This will help you better understand what you're going through, and equally as helpful, it'll show you what else is to come.

I sure hope you were honest with yourself in the second chapter. Don't feel ashamed to admit your relationship has a problem. After all, we *must* do this before we can start making positive changes. Hopefully, you identified the reason why communication has been less than great and you've finally been made aware of any mistakes you're currently making. But of course, don't just dwell on these problems. As I mentioned, you need to start creating better habits. You've learned all about the habits that save relationships. Start using these right away!

You've delved deeper into the many ways we can express and receive love. Once you've worked out what your partner's love language is, try and think of creative ways to show them how much you care. In fact, I highly recommend going over the section with them so you, too, can let your love language be known. When couples have a good understanding of each other's love languages, a lot less becomes lost in translation. Suddenly both partners are on the same page. Without all the confusion of trying to understand each other, they can just focus on the exchange of love.

While habits are certainly helpful, the two people at the core of the relationship must be healthy halves of the whole to really make it work. In order to form a great partnership and be a good partner, it's necessary that we learn to be emotionally healthy individuals. We don't become perfect once we enter into a relationship; all the emotional baggage and trauma we experienced beforehand comes with us! If we're not careful, past hurts can seep into our communication habits and tinge them with negativity. With the new tools you've been provided with, you can focus all your energy on becoming a better partner. You can finally start putting the past behind you. Try and help your partner do the same. At the end of the day, make sure you're meeting each others' needs – not just the five basic ones, but also the unique needs that come with their personalities.

Treat every sensitive situation with care. Know when you are dealing with a ticking time-bomb, and refer back to the relevant chapter for the techniques you need during the hard conversations. By following this guide closely, you'll ensure that even through the harsh storms, you always stay afloat. There is no such thing as completely smooth sailing in a relationship, but you can survive and make the most of the journey with these important tools. When we handle these situations the right way, they become opportunities for deeper intimacy. They become open doors instead of walls and dead-ends.

Relationship communication doesn't come naturally to anyone; it always takes work, commitment, and incredible self-discipline. It is a choice that loving partners make for each other everyday, and those that make the effort, reap rewards that others can scarcely imagine. Stay self-aware and do what you can to deepen your bond. Even people who are exceptionally close need to find time to maintain their connection. Let the love you foster through these lessons power every interaction from now on. I've shown you the wonderful path ahead, now it's your turn to walk it together.

www.ingramcontent.com/pod-product-compliance
Lightning Source LLC
Chambersburg PA
CBHW031121080526
44587CB00011B/1058